A Guide to Living Your *Creative Life*
Without Leaving Your Job

DO WHAT YOU LOVE

KATE VOLMAN

wellspring

Copyright © 2023 Kate Volman
PUBLISHED BY WELLSPRING
An Imprint of Viident

ISBN: 978-1-63582-333-2 (hardcover)
ISBN: 978-1-63582-332-5 (eBook)

Designed by Ashley Dias

10 9 8 7 6 5 4 3 2 1

FIRST EDITION

Printed in the United States of America

Dedication

*To my parents, who have always believed in me,
friends who support me,
mentors who challenge me,
and those who believe in their creativity
enough to show up and do the work.*

Table *of* Contents

Introduction

"I want to tell you something I've never told anyone before," a friend of mine whispered one evening while we were having dinner. We'll call him Brian.

"What?" I leaned in to find out his secret.

He took a deep breath and let it out. "I feel like I'm meant for more."

"What do you mean?" I asked.

"It just feels like something is missing." A painful expression crossed his face as he searched to put it into words. "I can't really describe it. I just know I'm meant for more."

Have you ever felt like Brian? Like there is something more for you if you could just figure out how to get there?

For most of us, our lives have not turned out the way we expected. In some ways, they are better than we imagined. However, in other ways, we find ourselves in situations we never imagined.

When we were young, most of us didn't worry about making poor decisions. We thought all of our ideas were brilliant.

We didn't ask permission to try something new. We jumped into puddles, colored pictures outside the lines, made new friends without hesitation, and had fun doing it. Over time, though, we may have stopped embracing the world with wide-eyed wonder, trading in our curiosity for the practical, safe, and responsible. And this pragmatic approach sucked away the joy that came with childlike wonder and play. Maybe that little voice in your head reminds you of the passions you have given up. It reminds you of the times you gave yourself permission to explore your **Creative Pursuits.**

Creative Pursuits are soulful activities that spark joy. They are your passion projects and creative ideas brought to life in whatever form calls you: singing, dancing, painting, writing, photography, video creation, programming, gardening, cooking, interior design, crafting, performing, fashion, or whatever makes you feel most alive. Your Creative Pursuits live inside you. Their job is to guide you toward a fulfilling life brimming with activities you love. But they can do their job only if they are nurtured and loved by you.

It is easy to respond to their call when we are young, but too often we give up our Creative Pursuits as more responsibilities fill up the free spaces in our lives. I see it all the time in my work. As the CEO of Floyd Coaching, I, along with my team, help people become the-best-version-of-themselves. We help them rediscover and achieve their dreams. Throughout my career, I have worked with hundreds of entrepreneurs, business owners, and professionals to help them grow. In addition to my work, I have launched podcasts, created videos, written for local and national publications, and produced online shows promoting interesting people and businesses. These are some of my Creative Pursuits.

I have seen firsthand the power of Creative Pursuits, not only in my career but also in the lives of the incredible individuals I serve. The common thread in all of these people is the need to express their creativity. It doesn't matter what industry they are in, what position they hold, where they live, how old they are, or their level of experience. If they are not plugged into their passions and creative ideas, they feel stuck and out of alignment.

Brian is an example of what happens when we are not plugged into our Creative Pursuits. He felt like something was missing. He got so lost in the busyness of work and life that he was no longer making time for his Creative Pursuits. He convinced himself that his dissatisfaction could be cured only by making more money, getting a new job, or acquiring more things. He was not sure what exactly could get him out of this rut.

As we talked that evening, he barely touched his meal. Swirling the straw in his glass of water, he gazed past me as if the future he was searching for could be found through the palm trees and twinkle lights hanging over the restaurant's patio bar.

That night I asked him one question worth asking ourselves when we lack the spark and fulfillment in our lives: "What do you love to do that you have stopped making time for?"

He paused for a few moments and then said, "Photography." He could spend hours watching video tutorials on how to get the right angle, how to pick the best times of day to shoot outdoors, and how to select the right lens to capture the details.

Photography has been a passion of his for years, but he convinced himself it was a waste of time. He was an adult, after all. He thought because he wasn't planning to make it his career, and knew he would never be the best, why bother?

"How was your life different when you made time for photography?" I asked.

Questioning how our lives are different when our Creative Pursuits are being explored is another great practice.

Brian knew immediately. "It was fun. I loved trying to get better each time I took pictures. It was kind of like a game."

After an engaging conversation about his love of the craft and why creativity matters, Brian decided to make photography part of his life again. He started bringing his camera to his favorite local coffee shop, outdoor concerts, and weekend trips to the green market downtown. He took more strolls during the week to find beautiful scenery to capture. He even signed up for a photography class. The more time he spent with his camera, the more engaged he became in other areas of his life. His energy and enthusiasm increased, not only when he was taking pictures, but at work, too. His team members, friends, and family started noticing his changed outlook. Suddenly he was more positive, more supportive, and more engaging. Photography opened his world to new people, places, and opportunities. His Creative Pursuit provided more than he expected.

He used to think making time for activities he enjoyed was a waste of time. Now he can't imagine not exploring his ideas and pursuing his passion projects. Not because they will make him rich. Not because they are a requirement. Simply because they bring him joy.

I have seen similar experiences happen to people over and over again. Without fail, when a client plugs into their passions, they become happier. I know that when I plug into my passions, I become happier. So, the real question is, do you want to be happier? If so, what is one Creative Pursuit you could indulge in today?

We feel unfulfilled when we don't create space in our lives to pursue our creativity. When we don't allow ourselves to feed our Creative Pursuits, our soul starves. We get that nagging sense that something is missing. When the nag comes, could it be our Creative Pursuits whispering to us to start exploring? Like a child tugging on your shirt trying to get your attention, your Creative Pursuits won't stop until you show them some love.

Why Do We Stop Exploring?

ONE REASON we stop exploring our Creative Pursuits is the abundance of messages we consume every day about what our life *should* look like. It's no wonder we start believing happiness exists only if we collect more things—a bigger house, a nicer car, better clothes, and expensive jewelry. Many of us are brainwashed into believing we need to have more and more to be happy, when it's actually the small things that make us happiest—spending time with family and friends, doing work that matters, helping others, achieving our dreams, and exploring our creativity. Our happiness expands when we spend time on our Creative Pursuits.

If you are resisting your Creative Pursuits, they are waiting for you to take the first step. The problem is they will grow impatient. They want to have fun. They are tired of all the seriousness of being an adult. They want to find out what is possible for you and wish you would stop ignoring them, stop doubting them, and instead follow their lead and explore. They want you to know that once you test out your ideas and open your heart, goodness will flow. You will start to feel lighter and smile more as you build a fulfilling life.

Moving forward is not always easy. Case in point: This book is one of *my* Creative Pursuits. It would have been easier for me not to write it. In fact, it is a dream I put off for over a decade. I spent ten years resisting a Creative Pursuit that was calling me nearly every day. I put it off because I thought I wasn't ready. I questioned my writing skills. I was scared nobody would read it—or worse, that everyone who did read it would hate it.

A friend of mine asked me why I needed to write this book. I didn't *need* to. Nobody told me to write it. Nobody was waiting around for it to come out. But I finally decided it was time for me to stop overthinking and finally share a message I truly believe in: *Following your Creative Pursuits leads to a more fulfilling life.* I believe this message will help someone feel more alive. I hope that someone is you.

I hope you discover whatever you need to make your Creative Pursuits a priority. I found that the pain of living with unfulfilled creativity inside me was greater than the fear and doubt that kept me from pursuing my passions. Once I got started writing, I couldn't stop. Believing that what I would share throughout these pages would inspire you to act on your Creative Pursuits helped me keep writing, even when I didn't feel like it.

That's one of the strange things about our Creative Pursuits. We love them, we are drawn to them, but sometimes they push us out of our comfort zone and challenge us to stretch our creativity muscle. Sitting down each day to write stretches my creativity. It isn't always easy for me. In fact, some days the resistance to writing burns a hole in my stomach. Resistance does everything it can to keep you busy with anything other than your Creative Pursuits—checking social media, calling a friend, searching online, or finally cleaning out your office. It knows how to distract you. And it never gets tired of telling you why you should put off your passions.

Fortunately, there is a way to overcome this powerful force: Start without judgment. When I push past resistance, sit at my desk, and start writing, creativity takes over. Even if what I create isn't any good, at least I'm taking the first step. Plus, I am doing what I love. It reminds me that I am in control, not some outside force doing its best to interfere with my happiness. Exploring my Creative Pursuits makes me a better person because I'm creating something that matters to me. Every time I write I gain a clearer understanding of who I am and who I'm meant to be. I can only become that person when I explore my creativity. The same is true for Brian with photography. The same is true for you and whatever you feel called to explore.

You reading this means you are ready to take action on the Creative Pursuits you have been thinking about for years but may have been putting off for just as long. In this book, I outline the seven myths stopping people from exploring their

Creative Pursuits and doing what they love. All of these myths have, at one point or another, kept me from pursuing my own creativity. Identifying them makes them easier to confront. Recognizing when we are allowing one of them to veer us off course helps us take the necessary actions to get back on our path to fulfillment.

Some of these myths will resonate with you more powerfully than others. Notice which ones those are. Be honest with yourself. Challenge yourself to think differently about the way you approach life. Doing so will help you break free of these myths and start living a more fully engaged and creative life.

Putting things off is the biggest waste of life: it snatches away each day as it comes, and denies us the present by promising the future. The greatest obstacle to living is expectancy, which hangs upon tomorrow and loses today.... The whole future lies in uncertainty: live immediately.

— Seneca[1]

Creativity Lives in You

YOU MAY NOT consider yourself to be creative, but creativity lives in each of us. Creativity is the way you show up at work, communicate in your relationships, play with your kids, approach a challenging situation, and, of course, pursue your passion projects. It's how you connect ideas and it's how you navigate the world.

Early in my career, I explored ideas that were interesting to me. I did not overthink my way out of taking a course, applying for an opportunity, attending a conference, or contacting an author whose work I enjoyed. But I didn't fully grasp the importance of creativity in my life. I didn't realize that pursuing passion projects unrelated to my job would not only bring me joy but would also help me become the person I am today.

That's what our Creative Pursuits do. They encourage us to explore what's interesting to us. When we do, we are invited to experience the challenges, joys, frustrations, and delight that build our skills and character and prepare us for the future we envision for ourselves. Your Creative Pursuits are unique to you. Embrace them. To some people, many of my Creative Pursuits may look like work. That's okay. I enjoy activities like writing, podcasting, and creating videos. I have friends who love gardening, graphic design, and jujitsu, none of which really interest me. Certain things are meant for me and others are meant for you. Each of us has our own creative calling. Our Creative Pursuits help us to fulfill that calling. When we have an idea, we use our creativity to execute it in a way that nobody else can. My dream for you is that you start making time for your Creative Pursuits. Those soulful activities that bring you joy are pure magic.

Rediscover Your Creative Pursuits

THEY ARE MAGIC because they help you discover more about yourself. Everything you have done up to this point in your life has helped you become the person you are today. All the blessings, failures, chance happenings, luck, hard work, relationships, challenges, and every moment in between helped you become . . . you. Maybe you're satisfied. Maybe you're not. Either way, you are not finished growing. You are not finished creating. Continue the journey by saying *yes* to your Creative Pursuits. *Yes* to the ideas and experiences you know are meant for you.

This book isn't about turning your passions into a business. If that's one of your aspirations, beautiful. These ideas will support you and that dream. But the real essence of this book is that exploring your Creative Pursuits will lead to a more fulfilling life. It is about helping you to explore your creativity, rediscover your passion projects, and give yourself permission to start. It is about doing what you love simply for the joy of it.

Not every creative idea needs to be monetized. In fact, the minute we exchange money for our creative projects, our relationship with that activity changes. The woman who turns her love of baking into a business. The artist who starts charging for his paintings, or the writer turned professional author. The carefree moments in the kitchen, playing in the studio, and creating stories just for fun are now attached to deadlines, responsibilities, and expectations. There's added pressure to the creative process that does not exist when it's simply meant for fun.

If you do turn one of your Creative Pursuits into a business, you will experience benefits in creating space for another one whose sole purpose is to bring you joy. One that switches your brain from work to play. From strategy and outcome to lighthearted fun. We all deserve to have fun. Life can be challenging. It can also be beautiful. We are built to create, experience, learn, support, love, fail, get up and try again, and grow. We are meant to live. You have everything you need inside you. I hope these ideas unlock your creativity and help you live a more fulfilling life.

We Are All Artists

We are all artists.
Not because we paint beautiful pictures or write poetry,
but because we care deeply about our craft and
choose to follow our dreams.
Our work is more than just an output of daily activities
that results in a paycheck.
Our work is about creation, contribution, exploration,
and making an impact.

It's the teacher staying late to help a student get better.

The programmer who never stops writing code.

The comedian who gets on stage every night
even when nobody laughs.

The hospital janitor who takes pride in an
immaculate operating room.

The entrepreneur who believes her idea
will change the world.

We are all artists when we follow our creative genius.

Your passion is not what you do.

It's how you breathe life into everything you pursue.

We are drawn to those who exude enthusiasm. They're like
a lighthouse shining brightly in the midst of a dark storm.

Their excitement is contagious. They inspire us to believe in
our ideas. To push when times are tough. To try even when it
feels impossible. To know that we always have more to give.

We are all artists.

We practice our craft.

We pursue greatness.

We fight mediocrity.

We live for small moments that ignite big ideas.

We believe in progress.

We love change more than we hate it.

We laugh at perfection.

We grow every day.

We praise our heroes.

We fall.

We cry.

We get up.

We laugh and keep going.

We build alliances.

We notice talent.

We embrace adversity.

We trust the process.

We pray for patience.

We hope for a masterpiece.

We are all artists because we continue to do the work.

Inspired Actions

It is too easy for us to read a book and not implement any of the ideas we have learned. This is why I have included Inspired Actions activities at the end of each chapter. They are meant to help you take action. Some of them are journaling prompts to help you discover more about yourself. Others are activities that may push you out of your comfort zone. I encourage you to use them so you can get the most out of this book.

Are you ready?
Here's to exploring, laughing, failing,
loving, discovering, crying, dreaming,
and continuing to do the work.
Here's to your *Creative Pursuits* journey.

Myth 1:
It's Not Possible

The Possible's slow fuse is lit
By the Imagination!
—Emily Dickinson[2]

IF TODAY WERE YOUR LAST DAY ON THIS PLANET, what would you regret not having tried?

Could you confidently say you lived your life fully for you?

What message would you wish you had shared with your father, mother, sister, brother, mentor, significant other, or best friend?

What would you have created?

Losing the Training Wheels

LET'S EXPLORE how children can teach us to shift our thinking and live more fully.

She pointed to the scrapes on her knees, which reminded her father of the last time she tried to ride her bike without training wheels.

Her father smiled.

She pouted. She was more concerned about letting her father down than she was about getting another scrape on her leg.

She hopped on the bike and started pedaling. She fell. She got up. She fell again.

Arms crossed, lips pursed, she stomped her foot on the sidewalk as she watched her older brother swoosh by on his bike with ease.

She brushed the grass off her purple shorts, jumped on the bike with a fierce look of determination, and pedaled.

Before she knew it, she had reached the blue house at the end of the cul-de-sac. She screamed in excitement, beaming with satisfaction as she continued gliding down the sidewalk. She stopped safely, turned around, and saw her father, hands in the air and smiling even more broadly than before.

Glowing with pride, she hopped back on the seat and started pedaling.

That child lives in each of us.

Unfortunately, many people drown her (or him) out over time.

They stop getting up after they fall. They stay on the ground defeated, staring at their scrapes and watching all the other bikes race by. They settle for training wheels. They settle for mediocrity. Life may not be as fun or as fulfilling, but at least they know what to expect. They play it safe, never venturing outside their comfort zone. They don't know what lives beyond the protected space they have created, and they are too scared to find out. Most people create a life they tolerate instead of one they love playing in, one filled with excitement, joy, happiness, and fulfillment.

Some people, on the other hand, are determined to lose the training wheels. They are committed to building a life overflowing with activities that light them up. A life filled with optimism and love. A life they are excited to step into each morning. They may not know exactly what to do to design that kind of life, but every day they jump on the bike and pedal.

Which kind of person are you? Do you stay on the ground, disengaged, or do you pedal?

For most of us, when we are young the world feels full of possibility. It never occurs to us that we can't become an astronaut, ballerina, scientist, or professor. We paint pictures, make up games, choreograph dances, and sing at the top of our lungs. We invent new ways to stay up past our bedtime and we never stop asking why. We live in a world of creativity, where anything is possible. We find many things interesting, and we want to explore them all.

As we get older, our world changes. *We* change. Over time, we start dealing with the realities of our messy life: losing a job, divorce, illness, caring for sick children or parents, losing a loved one, unexpected bills, heartbreak. Somewhere along the way many of us lose our carefree view of the world. We tell ourselves we can't dream when we have bills to pay and responsibilities to attend to.

But that is the very reason we should keep dreaming and exploring our Creative Pursuits. They ground us when things feel out of control. They provide moments of peace when everything else seems to be crumbling down around us.

Creative Pursuits remind us that we can live a more fulfilling life. If you were given a magic wand and could create the life of your dreams, what would it look like? How would you spend your days? Who would you spend time with? Where would you live? What would you do for a living? What organizations would you belong to? Where would you travel? What is stopping you from building that life?

You Control Your Happiness

MOST PEOPLE do not even try to get a little closer to that life because they do not believe it is possible to pursue their passions and achieve that kind of fulfillment. They believe they don't have the power to fight their external circumstances. They live with mantras like "If only" or "It is what it is." I am not fond of those phrases; they sound like we have given up.

Instead, what if we say something like "It is what you make

it"? Often, we have more power than we think we do to design a better life for ourselves. But we must first believe it is possible.

Too many of us spend more time thinking about why our ideas won't work than we do focusing on why they will. We pretend we don't have control of our happiness.

We convince ourselves our dreams don't matter, that they are unrealistic or unattainable. Dreams belong to children. Dreams belong to athletes. Dreams belong to celebrities and business moguls. Dreams, we tell ourselves, belong to everyone except us.

However, when we block out the noise and make space for our cluttered minds to settle and embrace silence, we hear that little voice reminding us of our power.

The voice pleads with us to believe we are meant for more. It asks us why we are fighting so hard for something we don't even want instead of focusing that energy on what it is we desperately do want. It encourages us to get back on the bike without the training wheels. It begs us to trust that it is worth it to start pedaling.

Now is your time to decide which of your voices you are going to listen to: the one starving to explore your creativity and passions, or the one that is constantly telling you it will never work. The voice convincing you that a mediocre life is all that is meant for you, or the voice of that brave little girl or boy who wants to get back on the bike after being knocked down.

Avoiding Happiness

A FRIEND of mine, we'll call him Patrick, had been working at the same company for over a decade. Every time we talked, he shared how stressed he was getting. While he did enjoy his job, each promotion he received added more responsibilities, managing different personalities, learning new skills, and strict deadlines. Longer hours and added stress also caused tension in his relationship with his girlfriend.

One afternoon, I received a call from him. He sounded really off.

"What's wrong?" I asked.

"Oh, I'm fine," he said sarcastically. "I just love working twenty-four-seven and fighting with my girlfriend."

I sighed. "Is it really that bad?"

"I'm just stressed. It feels like I'm working all the time. And when I'm not working, I just don't have the energy for anything else."

After a long pause, I asked, "When was the last time you played golf or went for a hike?"

"Are you kidding?" He laughed. "I can't remember the last time I even went to the driving range to hit balls."

"Can't you take one afternoon to go do something fun?"

"I don't know. It's fine. This is life. I don't want to talk about it," he said, defeated. "What's going on with you?" he asked, desperately trying to sound upbeat.

Patrick did not believe it was possible to have a better life. He settled for mediocrity because it was what he knew, and it got him by. He was miserable and unfulfilled but was not taking any steps to improve his circumstances. What saddened me most was believing how much Patrick's life would change for the better if he explored his Creative Pursuits.

He has always loved to draw, but it has been years since he took out his sketchbook. In fact, he stopped exploring most of his passions. He used to be so energetic and full of life, but now sadness fills his eyes. He wanted something more, but he was too scared to make even the smallest changes.

If we don't believe a certain outcome is possible, it's no wonder we stay exactly where we are. We feel no sense of hope or control. However, when we shift our mindset from the impossible to what's possible, outcomes that were once hidden are revealed, sitting in plain sight. Our perspective changes and a better life feels attainable. We start to approach situations and decisions differently. We think and act from a place of abundance instead of scarcity. And others notice.

They notice because most people go through life never exploring what interests them. They do not take steps toward their dream life. This leaves them watching others swoosh by on their bicycles, laughing, playfully reaching their hands to the sky, and enjoying the sunshine on their faces.

The good news is that today can be the day you make a different choice. Today can be the day you stop simply going through the motions of life and instead listen to your inner voice and tap into your creativity.

Going Through the Motions

MOST OF US are really good at going through the motions of daily life and having our checklist rule our lives. The problem lies in the fact that staying busy is our way of avoiding what matters. Staying busy keeps us from pursuing the things that bring us joy.

Owning your dreams and exploring your creativity takes commitment. We make the choice every day to either take one step toward achieving our dreams or turn our back on them. The path of our big ideas is filled with the unknown, while the responsible path seems protected—which is why we often choose the latter. However, it turns out *both* paths are filled with uncertainty. But only the path with our passions is sprinkled with the magic that empowers us to become who we are meant to be. When we allow ourselves to loosen up and start believing we can create a better life, the steps to get there are revealed.

Which path are you choosing right now?

The Decision Only You Can Make

ONE OF my clients, Sarah, had to choose which path she would take when she finally decided to explore one of her Creative Pursuits. During one of our sessions, she shared her dream of writing a book. Her eyes widened and her smile brightened as she described what the book would be about.

I asked how far along she was in the process. She gazed at the floor. Her shoulders sank as she admitted to not having started. I asked her why.

"Well, I don't know how to write a book. Plus, I don't even know if it's a good idea. I'm so busy with work and—"

"So, you're talking yourself out of it before you even start?" I interrupted.

She laughed. "Yeah, I guess that's exactly what I'm doing."

"Do you believe it's possible for you to write a book?"

She looked at me and said, "Yes."

"Are you ready to choose you?"

Silence filled the room as I waited for her answer.

"I don't know," she said softly, almost ashamed.

I asked her to clarify.

"I don't know if I can do that. It sounds selfish," she said.

"Selfish? What do you mean by that?"

Sarah told me about yoga, writing, and other passions she had given up over the years. She could not justify taking time away from her family or work. She had convinced herself she did not deserve these things.

I asked her to reflect on and journal about the feelings that showed up when she heard the phrase "Choose you." I also invited her to consider the possibility that choosing Sarah could very well be the best thing she could do for herself, her family, and her work.

If your response to the question "Are you ready to choose you?" is similar to Sarah's, I urge you to do the same journaling exercise. This is a question only you can answer—and a decision only you can make. It is worth spending some time on because you matter.

I often recommend journaling exercises to my friends and clients. There is something powerful about getting your thoughts out of your head and onto the page. Journaling is a form of meditation. It is a way to discover more about yourself and what you truly want. For me, it is a creative practice. The more I journal, the more ideas I generate, and the more confident I become in exploring my creativity and choosing myself.

Choosing you is not selfish. It means believing in your ideas. It means believing your Creative Pursuits will lead you toward a more fulfilling life. Choosing you means you are ready to take action. It means giving yourself permission to start doing more of what you love. Choosing you means saying *yes* to your creativity, *yes* to your ideas, and *yes* to becoming the person you are destined to be.

The passion in your heart to achieve greatness is there for a reason. Greatness does not necessarily mean being rich and famous. It does not necessarily mean being an entrepreneur or business mogul. It means fulfilling your own highest potential in areas that matter to you.

What does greatness mean to you? Having the flexibility to spend time with your family and friends? Being part of a team doing great work? Being an incredible parent, friend, or sibling? Creating something only you can create? Whatever it is, it should light you up. Giving yourself permission to pursue the ideas that light you up and fill you with joy will lead you on your path to greatness, whatever that looks like to you.

Do you believe it's possible to become the person you want to be? The person who takes the first step? The person who believes in their creativity enough to move beyond their comfort zone? The person who actively explores their Creative Pursuits? If your answer is *yes*, then you are ready to choose you.

Step Beyond Your Fears

We have the opportunity to choose ourselves for what we long to do at different times throughout our lives. In high school, if you gave me a basketball, I would be the first to run out on the court. Throw me a pair of goggles and I would jump in the pool and start swimming. But ask me to get up in front of the class to give a presentation and I would pull the covers over my head and beg my mom to let me stay home from school that day. Like many people, I hated public speaking. And I do mean *hated*. I can still remember the burning sensation in my cheeks as the blood rushed to my face every time I stood in front of my classmates.

I did not think it was possible to get over this fear. When I discovered that public speaking was a mandatory class in college, I cringed. I just wanted it to be over so I could move on with my audience-free life. It was a mystery how anyone enjoyed this horrifying activity. I gritted my teeth, passed the course, and hoped I would never have to give another speech again.

Unfortunately, it seemed as though situations that provoked this fear of mine were unavoidable. I was required to present in many other college classes throughout my four years. I also ended up in front of a few crowds at the start of my career. While I may have gotten a bit more comfortable, it did not seem to get any easier.

It was like this until years later when I was working at a chamber of commerce. One morning my boss informed me that he was unable to attend our luncheon later that day and that I would have to emcee it. Mortified, that afternoon I found myself standing in front of over one hundred leaders at the event. Heart pounding and hands shaking, I stood at the podium, microphone in hand, staring at the crowd. Nervous, but ready to get it over with, I opened the meeting with a joke. Laughter filled the room.

That moment changed my life.

I spoke, they laughed. Again and again, I played in a relationship with the audience. The knot in my stomach loosened. I looked at their smiling faces and all I wanted was to provide more entertainment. As I continued speaking, I found I was actually having fun being fully myself and engaging with the audience. It felt so natural. Their laughter encouraged me. I fell in love with speaking while connecting with my audience that day.

What once felt impossible now felt right, as if I were living my purpose.

Full disclosure: Over the years I have spoken at hundreds of events and still get nervous before taking the stage or speaking to a large group. But every time I do, I learn something. I get better. The nervousness reminds me of the possibilities ahead. It reminds me that if I believe something is both important and possible, I will figure it out. Or at the very least I will have fun trying.

Actions Follow Beliefs

ALTHOUGH I didn't know it at the time, that moment at the luncheon changed me. I felt more confident, accepted, and excited to uncover more opportunities to use my gifts.

From that moment forward, I was convinced that creativity lives in all of us. I started noticing the unique talents of my coworkers, chamber members, and friends. I watched as entrepreneurs used their business savvy to fundraise at events, friends made jewelry to give as special gifts, and coworkers turned their love of numbers into easy-to-use spreadsheets.

Sometimes we use our creativity to directly support the work we do. Sometimes, we use it to explore pieces of ourselves simply because exploring makes us feel alive.

Your Creative Pursuits can be anything. For some it's drawing, photography, fashion, or interior design, while for others it's cooking, dancing, or glassblowing. And of course, you can have more than one. You may have buckets of Creative Pursuits that excite you. Explore all the ideas you find interesting and discover which ones make your heart sing loudest.

Once you do, you will find that creativity lives everywhere. Everything you feel called to explore is a host of surprising new adventures that can broaden your outlook on the world and change how you show up in your life. Examining these passions can open the floodgates to countless new possibilities you would not have uncovered otherwise.

These passions infuse our lives with inspiration to keep exploring, to have more fun, and to live with deeper gratitude. When we believe in our ideas, we give ourselves permission to try. We worry less about failing and focus more on living. The walls of doubt start to crumble each time we do something that supports one of our Creative Pursuits. With each step, we find it easier to take action. And with each new action, our confidence builds.

Believing It's Possible

WITH EACH new action, our belief grows stronger. It's the single woman who does not believe it is possible to find love—until she musters up the courage to start dating again. The frustrated employee who almost gives up on finding a better job—until he starts a conversation with an entrepreneur launching a cool new start-up, who asks for his résumé. The anxious, overworked CEO who believes happiness exists only in some distant future—until dance lessons become a weekly activity that immediately brings more joy to her life and business. The girl who believes she's too young to start a business—until she finds a mentor who helps her take the first step.

The world is full of businesses, inventions, art, music, poetry, shows, comedy, entertainment, dances, recipes, and ideas that may have once seemed impossible, until the creators brought their ideas to life. They believed in the possibility of a future nobody else could see. They did not allow what they *couldn't* do to interfere with what they *could*. They believed in their idea enough to try, not knowing the outcome.

Happiness and joy are available to you. Not tomorrow. Not ten years from now. Today. Right now. Believing it is possible is just the beginning. Belief can unlock possibilities or lock in mediocrity.

Six Questions That Will Change Your Life

1. WHAT BELIEFS are holding you back from pursuing the life you want?
2. What truly makes you happy?
3. What really matters to you?
4. What are your dreams?
5. In what ways have you settled for mediocrity?
6. What would taking action on your dreams look and feel like?

It's easy to gloss over these questions. You may promise to think about them later, but there is no better time than now. Maybe you are scared to face your answers. They may reveal emotions you have spent years avoiding. Consider taking time to sit with these questions and allow yourself to feel the emotions they bring up for you. The answers will reveal what you most likely already know but may not have fully admitted to yourself just yet. They may be exactly what you need to start building a life you love.

The Power of Starting

WE NEVER know what's on the other side of starting. Even the best, most deeply thought-through plans go in directions we could never have imagined. The unpredictability is exciting. It's scary. It's beautiful. It's messy.

Believing in possibilities is the key to harnessing the incredible power of starting. Once we believe, we focus less on outcome, more on process. Less on doubt, more on faith. Less on fear, more on possibility. Don't wait until you have all the answers. Starting uncovers them.

You don't have to see the whole staircase,
just take the first step.
—Martin Luther King Jr.[3]

Your Future Self

THINK OF your ideal future self. The one who is confident, believes in your ideas, approaches life with optimism, and always keeps pedaling. What advice would this future version of you share with you today? Mine tells me to keep showing up. Keep doing the work even when it's hard—especially when it's hard. My future self reminds me that it is moments of difficulty that give me the strength I need to believe in my ideas and pursue my passions. When we keep showing up and pursuing our passions, we start seeing evidence that supports our efforts. They are like little prizes we get to collect after a job well done.

Look for Evidence

MY FRIEND Jenn found a great prize in the following story.

One afternoon, I received a call from her.

"There are no good men out there!" she yelled before I even had a chance to say hello.

"Here we go," I laughed.

She had been single for about two years and really wanted to be in a relationship. She was not enjoying dating and had convinced herself she would never find a good man.

She ranted for a few minutes before I interrupted. "Tell me about a guy you had a nice time with."

Her breath caught. "What?"

I repeated myself.

After a few minutes of silence, she told me about Peter. He took her downtown for a walk and they ended up having lunch at one of her favorite restaurants.

"He's a nice guy, but I wasn't interested in him romantically."

"Okay," I said. "But he's a nice guy?"

"He really is."

"Who else do you consider great men in your life?"

Jenn told me about a good friend, a coworker she confides in, and her friend's husband.

"So, are there good men out there?" I asked.

"Okay, okay," she said reluctantly. "I see where you're going with this."

"And you just have to find one of them. Why not enjoy getting to know interesting people and new experiences until you find him?" I asked enthusiastically.

Jenn had put blinders on, so she missed the evidence that there are good men. When we tell ourselves there are no good partners, jobs, or opportunities, that is what we see and experience. We will find evidence that supports those ideas. When we open ourselves up to possibility, a funny thing happens: More possibilities start showing up.

Our job is to look for evidence that supports our dreams. If you focus on all the reasons your life will be better when you make time for your Creative Pursuits, they will become obvious. On the other hand, if you focus on the reasons you shouldn't make that time, you will find plenty of those, too. If you want to find evidence that supports your Creative Pursuits, think about a time you did something you love just for fun.

When we play with our passions, naturally we become a better spouse or partner, friend, mother, boss, son, mentor, or team member because we are having more fun and our needs are being met. There is lots of evidence hidden throughout your daily life that supports your creativity. The more you believe it is possible to create a fulfilling life, the easier it will be to do so.

Inspired Actions

Whether you know what Creative Pursuits you would like to follow or you are not quite sure, brainstorming helps generate ideas. The following activities will help you (1) prepare your mindset and strengthen your belief system, and (2) identify at least one Creative Pursuit you are excited to start exploring.

1. Identify at least one activity that used to feel impossible but is now part of your life (e.g., waking up early, playing piano, working out regularly, networking at events).
2. What beliefs are currently holding you back from exploring your Creative Pursuits?
3. List one to three ways you will choose you this week (e.g., make time for one of your Creative Pursuits, say no to thoughts that do not serve you, share your ideas, learn a new skill).
4. Create a list of the top ten Creative Pursuits you would like to work toward. If you're stuck and need some inspiration, ask a friend to create their list with you. Here are a few ideas to get you started: cooking, poetry, photography, singing, dancing, painting, designing, martial arts, and crafting. Have fun.

Myth 2:
You're Not Good Enough

Belonging starts with self-acceptance. Your level of belonging, in fact, can never be greater than your level of self-acceptance, because believing that you're enough is what gives you the courage to be authentic, vulnerable and imperfect.

—Brené Brown[4]

A FEW YEARS INTO MY CAREER, I started a business running events and mastermind programs to support women entrepreneurs. I reconnected with Yvonne, a well-respected and influential woman in the community.

I asked if she had any advice for my first entrepreneurial adventure.

"Kate, I'm surprised," she answered. "I thought you were here to ask for my business."

My face turned red. Of course I wanted her business. That was exactly what I had come for, but my insecurities had stopped me.

Who was I to ask this extremely successful woman to do business with me? No matter how much I had accomplished up to that point, unworthiness suffocated my confidence. I was still trying to prove myself to my colleagues, my family, prospective clients, and countless others who were not questioning my worth. *They* were not thinking I wasn't enough. *I* was.

Some people can spend a lifetime collecting experiences and winning awards yet never feel worthy, full, and whole. We may find ourselves minimizing our own accomplishments while at the same time praising others for what they have achieved.

Although I did ultimately ask Yvonne for her business, we never ended up working together. Fortunately, I received something even better that day. I learned how to step into my power and believe I am enough.

You Are Not an Impostor

I WALKED into Yvonne's office feeling like a complete fraud, believing that I needed more experience, more knowledge, and more business savvy before someone at her level of success would work with me. But that was a self-inflicted issue. When we feel as though something is missing, achieving a sense of worthiness from within can be difficult.

Have you ever felt that way? Scared that one day someone is going to find out you are not as good as everyone thinks you are? That you are not worthy of your role, your accomplishments, or pursuing your dreams?

If so, you are not alone. About 70 percent of the population experiences this intense creativity-crushing feeling at some point in their lives.[5] Sometimes we disregard our accomplishments and convince ourselves our success must have been a fluke. As a result, we are constantly peering over our shoulders, petrified that someone is going to discover we do not belong here. This debilitating experience is called impostor syndrome.[6]

Impostor syndrome places roadblocks between us and our passions. When you are trying something new, it may be challenging not to feel like an impostor. The first steps toward your Creative Pursuits can be scary when you are venturing into unknown territory. But that is the very place you gain the confidence and skills to help you improve. Plus, you have managed to figure things out in the past, which means you can do it again with new experiences. When we are comfortable with who we are today, we explore our passions with more confidence and intention. Remember, you have nothing to prove to anyone.

You have to be where you are to get where you need to go.
—Amy Poehler[7]

Nothing to Prove

TRYING TO prove our worth to others can be exhausting. We may have convinced ourselves our worthiness lives on the other side of our next accomplishments. When we get the promotion, buy the nicer car, land a big client, or make a certain amount of money, that's when everything will fall into place and we will feel fulfilled.

The problem is, every time we achieve one goal, we are already thinking about what is next. This brings more anxiety, doubt, and stress. We can get caught up in thinking the next milestone has to be bigger than the last. We often don't even make time to celebrate the win before moving on to the next goal. Celebration is important, and too often, we ignore it. Embrace your wins.

You can't earn worthiness—you already have it. You are perfectly fabulous just as you are.

What a relief, huh?

I find that when I accept I am good enough and believe I am exactly who and where I am meant to be right now, I approach every task with more lightness, more fun, and yes, more joy, because I am good as is. I strive to approach every experience, opportunity, and relationship with gratitude, confidence, and humility, trusting that I am enough. And you are, too.

If you are dealing with impostor syndrome, try these three actions:

1. Acknowledge your feelings and recognize that you are not alone.

2. Create a Victory Vault. List all of your proudest accomplishments. You can keep them in a file on your computer, write them down in a notebook, or glam up an old shoebox with glitter and ribbons. However you decide to track your wins, remember to tap into your vault when you need a reminder of how incredible you are.

3. Do a self-talk check in. Notice the messages you are sending yourself. If they are negative, you know what to do: Shut them down and switch to positive messages. Your Creative Pursuits will be so proud.

Embrace Your Power

ANOTHER WAY to fight impostor syndrome is to simply, fully embrace your power, even when you don't quite feel it. A friend of mine, Becca, used to sell brightly colored shirts with "I am" statements on them. *I am brave. I am love. I am abundant. I am enough.*

One day she received a request from a woman asking her to create shirts featuring "be" statements instead. *Be brave. Be confident. Be enough.*

Becca asked why.

The woman told her she did not feel comfortable wearing a shirt making such bold "I am" statements because she did not yet feel that way.

That woman could not even wear a shirt proclaiming, "I am enough." Think about that.

How would you feel wearing those words across your chest? I hope you would wear them proudly, believing you are enough.

You are not your job, your age, your academics, your social status, your popularity, your social media following, or your relationship status. You are so much more than these things. You are a creative human being. You are unique, complex, messy, lovable, and filled with emotion. You are here for a reason. You have an obligation to set your own course in life. You are enough exactly as you are.

Say these words out loud, right now:

I am enough.

Say it again, more powerfully.

I am enough.

It may seem silly, but sometimes a reminder is what we need to keep showing up. To keep pedaling.

Notice what happens to your body and mind when you say those words. How does it make you feel? Maybe you feel empowered and confident. If so, amazing! Say these words when you need a boost of courage. You might feel a little uncomfortable because you do not fully believe them yet. If that's the case, repeat them to yourself multiple times a day. Each time will break through a layer of doubt until you uncover the confidence waiting to be unleashed. It may be covered up with past failures and heartbreak, but it's there. You will get it back.

Words Can Lift You Up or Tear You Down

IT'S IMPORTANT to pay close attention to the words you use when talking about yourself. Some of us are quick to praise others but are not as kind to ourselves. Some of us encourage our friends to pursue their passions but do not go after our own. We can be our friends' biggest cheerleaders and our own worst bullies.

Here are some disempowering words that can show up in our internal dialogue.

I can't . . .

I'll never . . .

I'm not good enough . . .

Consider how different these words feel:

I can . . .

I will . . .

I am more than enough . . .

I witnessed just how powerful changing our internal dialogue is with my brilliant writer friend, Nathan. The first time I read one of his poems, the words jumped out and touched my soul with the elegance and beauty he creates with captivating images and with his truths.

In fact, it was reading his work that led me deeper down the path of loving poetry.

But I was one of the only people he shared his work with. Surprised, I asked him why.

"Nobody wants to read this stuff," he scoffed.

This incredible writer didn't think his work was good enough. How could that be? His words had changed my view of the world and inspired me to explore my creativity. So I became the nagging friend who begged him to share his work with others.

This went on for years. He would send me short, brilliant poems about love, regret, passion, or pandas. I would encourage him to share them with others. I would tell him the world needed to read his work.

I could tell he *wanted* to share his writing with a bigger audience. In fact, he promoted articles and other pieces he wrote for his day job and people really enjoyed them. It was his creative writing that he kept closer to his chest.

Finally, I asked if I could share one of his poems with a few friends. His work was unique, and I thought the group would appreciate it.

Reluctantly, he agreed.

When I told him how much my friends enjoyed it, he was touched and surprised. I think he was secretly bracing for the worst. But because the feedback was good, he kept writing, with even more intensity. And little by little, he started sharing, first in front of small groups, then larger crowds. And then he published his own book of poems, which received rave reviews.

Did it bother him if someone did not like them? Sure. It stung, but at that point, he cared more about his work than about the critics. He believed his voice mattered and that the right people would find it.

Care More About Your Passions Than About the Haters

THE MORE Nathan shared his work, the stronger his confidence grew. Your ideas can find their place only when you are pursuing them. Unfortunately, when we start taking action on our passions, some people will not be very encouraging or kind. In fact, sometimes it is those closest to us who may get upset when they see us making time for our Creative Pursuits. Colleagues, friends, or even family members may discourage you from pursuing your passions and creativity. They may get uncomfortable watching you pursue your passions because they will be forced to admit they are not pursuing theirs. Their discouragement says more about them than it does about you.

People committed to pursuing their passions and creativity rarely criticize others for doing the same. They know the challenges and understand the mental toughness needed to keep showing up for yourself. To push even when it's hard. To fight the resistance and go all in on what it is you really want.

It is the people who are not exploring their Creative Pursuits who may judge you for following your heart. Do not let that judgment change your direction. Protect your ideas, your passions, and your Creative Pursuits by surrounding yourself with people who believe in you.

Supportive Friends

SURROUND YOURSELF with positive, supportive people. People who see your potential, support your ideas, and believe in your dreams. People who push you to explore what you know is meant for you.

Among my top supportive friends are my mother and father. Yes, I know they are my parents and that is in the job description. But still, I am incredibly blessed to have great ones. They have always been very supportive of my passion projects, even when they did not understand why I poured so much energy into them. They have listened to me ramble on for hours about my podcasts, videos, project ideas, and of course, writing this book. They build me up when I am not feeling great. For that, I am forever grateful.

Creative Friends

IN ADDITION to supportive friends, it is also helpful to surround yourself with others who are exploring their Creative Pursuits. Not only are they supportive, but they probably also understand the challenges you may be facing as you pursue your passions. It is likely they, too, have had to overcome some of the myths in this book, so they recognize what you are dealing with and can cheer you on. These are **Creative Friends.**

One of my Creative Friends, Anthony, called me while I was driving home from work one evening. We don't talk often, but when we do it is always a lively conversation about the creative projects we are working on.

This time, Anthony needed encouragement. He was feeling down because he'd left his job in pursuit of something new but had not found anything yet. He was frustrated and anxious.

One of his Creative Pursuits is improv comedy and sharing hilarious jokes and stories online. But I hadn't seen any lately, so I asked him why.

He sighed. "I haven't felt motivated to create anything. And honestly, I don't even know if the videos I do are even funny."

"What?" I yelled. "They're so good! And you *love* making them!"

"I'm just bummed, but I'll get over it," he said.

"What are some of the ideas you have?" I asked.

We immediately started brainstorming and he completely

forgot about his melancholy mood as we laughed at some of his ideas.

Later that week, he sent me an absolutely hilarious video he had created. Not only did it make me laugh, but seeing him get back into his creativity brightened my day.

Creative Friends are the best for shifting us back to our creativity. They are also good at reminding us to stop doubting ourselves and why we are passionate about our Creative Pursuits. The joy is found in the creation process, not the result. We will talk more about this in later chapters.

A bonus to having many Creative Friends is they all meet different needs. I call Kyle when I need to be challenged, Jeremy or Becca when I need encouragement, and Victoria or Wendi when a brainstorming session is a must.

If you are wondering who your Creative Friends are, here are five questions to ask to identify them:

1. Who always encourages you to pursue your dreams and passions?
2. Who inspires you because they are always pursuing their dreams and passions?
3. Who makes you feel seen and heard?
4. Who inspires you to take action after a conversation?
5. Who do you crave talking to because they fill you with energy?

Once you have identified your Creative Friends, let them

know how much you appreciate them. Schedule regular creative conversations to catch up and talk about your Creative Pursuits.

Better Every Day

CREATIVE FRIENDS can be found everywhere, and they are always looking for ways to grow. I used to work out at an amazing gym. The founders are incredible entrepreneurs who really care about their members. Their creativity was expressed in making every fitness class an experience, with music blasting, trainers screaming, and a group of fitness enthusiasts ready for their next physical challenge.

To enhance the experience, they put all over the black walls of the gym inspirational phrases like "Better Every Day." That one spoke to me the most. Isn't it great? We each have an opportunity to do better. We can begin again each day. A new day. A new chance to be a better friend, spouse, team member, entrepreneur, activist, musician, teacher, listener, coach, creator, mechanic, or leader. Each day we can leave our past behind and create a better future for ourselves and those in our circle of influence.

Make Your Future Self Proud

YOUR FUTURE self is cheering for you to get better every day. Imagine it's three years from today. You have been selected to receive a prestigious award, and one of your closest friends gets to present it to you.

Write the introduction they will share with the audience before inviting you up:

- What is the award for?
- What words do they use to describe you?
- What qualities do they appreciate about you?
- How have you impacted their life and the lives of others?

Writing this introduction is an opportunity for you to envision the kind of person you want to become. After you write it, take time to read through it and notice how it makes you feel. Live into those words.

Treasures in Exploring Unexpected Creative Pursuits

WE CAN find really cool treasures while exploring unexpected Creative Pursuits. One of my unexpected Creative Pursuits is poetry. Poetry did not interest me when I was younger. In fact, when my high school English teacher asked for my thoughts on Edgar Allan Poe's "The Raven," all I could do was mumble some nonsense words, just enough to prove I'd read it, but not quite enough to convince him I understood what it meant.

My bearded teacher took off his glasses and shook his head in annoyance, calling on someone else, who had a better sense of the treasures that could be found in that poem. That encounter left me believing that I was a hopeless cause when it came to poetry.

But poetry had a different idea. It kept showing up at unexpected times, inviting me into a world of strong emotions and whispering for me to question its meaning.

Poetry won me over by stirring my soul, causing me to grow curious about what the author was thinking when they penned certain phrases. Where were they when they wrote their best work? What inspired them? What was the story behind the story? I may never know for sure, but it is fun to think about.

Poetry hasn't unfolded all its secrets yet, but the secrets it has confessed have transformed me into a better writer and a more creative person.

Earlier, I mentioned my friend Nathan's poetry. Noticing my interest in his work, he encouraged me to write some of my own. I started writing poems for fun, but then Nathan began nagging me to share them. If he could find the courage, he argued, I could, too. Fair enough. Oh, the power of Creative Friends.

Although I was quite nervous, I did read my work publicly to a small group of creators, and it was exhilarating. When I was finished, I realized it didn't matter how good or bad my poem was. Poetry didn't care. It just wanted to be shared. That experience helped me realize that my work is good enough and that there is a place for my ideas. There is a place for yours, too.

Inspired Actions

1. Write the speech your friend will give about you before you accept your fabulous award. Don't hold back. It may feel a little uncomfortable. Good. That means you are including what is meant to be in it. Read it to yourself out loud. How does it make you feel?

2. Identify at least one Creative Friend. Schedule a creative conversation with them to discuss your Creative Pursuits and how you can support each other.

3. Start creating your Victory Vault. Write down all the accomplishments you are most proud of—receiving a promotion, trying something new, landing a big client, losing weight, having a successful marriage, being a supportive friend, achieving a dream, and everything you are most proud of accomplishing so far.

Myth 3:
You Need Permission

Everything is a choice. This is life's greatest truth
and its hardest lesson.

—Matthew Kelly[8]

HUNDREDS OF PROFESSIONALS IN DRESSES AND SUITS MINGLED with colleagues at a networking breakfast. Squeezing through the crowd, I bumped into Ryan, the owner of the local newspaper. Although we had never met, I knew who he was, and I had an idea I wanted to share with him. His newspaper featured great stories, but I felt it would be more impactful if they were shared through video.

"Hey, I know you," I said, smiling.

He laughed. "I know you, too."

"I've been meaning to reach out. Can we get together?" I said excitedly.

He handed me his business card. "Of course."

A few days later, I was sitting in his office sharing my idea of producing a live morning show to feature Delray Beach,

Florida, the beautiful city where we both lived and worked. It is an adorable, eclectic place with boutique shops, amazing restaurants, and interesting people.

"Imagine a weekly video show highlighting nonprofit organizations, people, and companies that are doing incredible work in our community," I said, creating the picture for him. "This would give a face and bring to life the work you are doing with your newspaper."

"Love it!" he said.

"Oh, and you would be my cohost," I added.

His face paled. "Um, that sounds like way too much work for me personally to get involved."

"Don't worry. We'll start small." I held up my phone and waved it. "All we need is a smartphone, a tripod, and a few guests to get things rolling."

His brow crinkled. "Where would we even shoot it?"

I jumped up from the couch and pointed to it. "Right here."

"Okay," he chuckled. "Let's try one episode and see what happens."

A week later, we were sitting on the orange couch, coffee mugs in hand, ready for our first show. One of Ryan's team members, Alexis, sat behind the tripod and camera while the rest of his team sat at their desks in the open-plan office, unsure of what to expect.

One Wednesday morning at eight thirty, Alexis pressed the

"go live" button.

Ryan and I welcomed the viewers, hoping we had some. Smiling, we shared our vision for this positive and community-oriented show and invited them to join us for this new journey.

When we were finished, Ryan looked at me, beaming. "That was really fun."

"You were so good!" I yelled. "Are you excited for the next one?"

"Actually, I am. And I have the perfect guest," he said.

What followed were hundreds of episodes, impromptu videos, and guest appearances at events. We even rocked the runway at a few fashion shows. It was an incredibly impactful couple of years. I met fabulous people, learned more about my community, and helped businesses and nonprofit organizations gain exposure.

There's something so magical about bringing an idea to life, not knowing where it will lead but being excited to find out. That is the fun of exploring our ideas. Inviting creativity into our everyday lives creates life-changing opportunities and experiences.

The show was simply an idea I wanted to explore. I could have kept it hidden inside and waited for someone to ask me to host a show. But we both know the chances of that happening.

When we have an idea that we can't stop thinking about, it is our responsibility to bring it to life. We can't wait for permission to start. We can't wait for someone else to put in the work and bring our idea to life. Nor can we wait for someone else to recognize our brilliance.

All you need to get started is a splash of courage.

Many people think courage is synonymous with swords and armor and no shred of fear. In truth, it is simply taking one first step *despite* our fears. That's it. And the good news is you have everything you need to take one small step. Besides, having the courage to start is the only way to discover what's on the other side of your idea.

I didn't know the impact our show would have on my life and the community when I started. You don't know what's on the other side of your Creative Pursuits before you start. But it is pretty sensational to go through the process to find out.

Our Happiness Expands to the Level of Our Courage

If you haven't started…

If you are still just gathering up the courage to invite creativity as a daily companion, think about this.

Take Your Power Back

What if you were enjoying a beverage at your favorite local restaurant and a stranger sat down next to you and whispered, "Starting today, you are no longer allowed to pursue your passions"?

You would probably laugh them off. Who are they to tell you what you can and can't do? You would not give them that kind of power over your life.

Why, then, are we sometimes that stranger, prohibiting ourselves from pursuing our dreams? We can choose to do more of what we love right now, yet most people choose to relive the same day over and over, hiding their passions and waiting for permission to explore them. No wonder so many people feel lost.

You may be ignoring your Creative Pursuits, but they are waiting patiently for you to discover the power they have to change your life. They know the magic that unfolds when you are brave enough to take the initiative, give yourself permission, and start.

Stop "Shoulding" Your Creativity Away

ONE WAY you might be giving your creative power away is by being too focused on what you think you *should* be doing instead of what you actually want to do.

A simple trick to identify if this is showing up in your life is to create a list of all the things you think you should do, think, or be. Your list may include ideas like:

- "I should have a bigger home."
- "I should take the corporate job."
- "I should be more successful."

- "I should be more social."
- "I should start an online business."
- "I should be in a relationship by now."

You may actually want to achieve some of these examples, which is great because you can choose to go after them. There is a different energy between *should* and *want to*. Many people add items to their "should" list even though it is not what they truly want. It's what their parents, friends, or colleagues convince them they should want, which often leads us to spending more time contemplating what we "should" do rather than listening to our heart and focusing on what we actually want. Our "shoulds" are influenced by outside sources or by us putting pressure on ourselves to be something we really do not want to be. Our passions spark from within.

Your "shoulds" don't make it onto your to-do list because you want them there. They usually end up there after you've read an article, watched a video, heard a message on a podcast, or been told by a friend they have the answers to make your life better.

And now the long list of things you "should" do leaves little to no room for the activities you actually *want* to do. You convince yourself that your passions are unrealistic and unattainable, but you make time for activities that don't interest you because you feel you have to, activities that might make sense for others but don't make sense for you.

As a coach, one commonality I see among many of my clients is they have abandoned at least one Creative Pursuit and it is making them miserable. They somehow find time for others, but not for themselves. Their calendars are filled with meetings, dinners, playdates, baseball games, errands, friends' parties, and everything else that is expected of them. What's missing, however, is yoga, hiking, baking, drawing, dance lessons, golf, or even a simple time block for doing nothing.

We say yes to events we would rather not attend because we do not want to upset friends. We agree to activities and functions we have no interest in to stay in good graces with colleagues. Other people's priorities replace our own until there is no space left for activities we love. It's no wonder we feel as though something is missing.

Your Creative Pursuits are not a nicety; they are an essential part of becoming your best self.

When we stop trying to gain the approval of others, doing what we love becomes easier. We start not because we received permission from others, but because we gave ourselves permission to choose ourselves and just go for it.

Nobody else holds the key to unlocking your potential. Don't wait for permission. Grant it yourself. Come on. You can do it. I dare you. You won't regret it.

We rarely regret pursuing our ideas. It's the ideas we don't pursue that we regret. All you have to do is say, "Yes, I am just as important as everyone else. Yes, my ideas matter and I have the right to pursue my dreams."

It's that simple.

Believe it. Sometimes we are our own worst critic. You know that dream-killing inner critic who whispers, "You are not good enough" or "You are not worthy," or asks, "Who do you think you are?" That voice gets louder and louder, hoping to convince you to give up before you even start.

But you are not going to let that happen because you have made the decision to go for it. And you are too tough to let anything stop you from pursuing your passions and building a life you love.

Wouldn't it be amazing if every passion project we pursued included a guarantee? A tiny gold seal of approval that your idea is good and that it will work? Pursuing anything would be easier if we knew we could not fail.

While that simply isn't how life works, we do get to roll the dice, make the first move, and see what happens. Besides, if you try, you win! It's guaranteed because you put yourself and your Creative Pursuits first, and in the end, that is what matters.

The only way to lose is by not trying. We choose to sit on the couch and watch TV or to get up and exercise. We choose to call a friend to gossip or to reach out to a mentor to have an inspiring conversation. We choose to scroll through social media or to practice the guitar.

These choices may seem insignificant at the time, but they add up every day, until you realize each one played a part in curating the life you are living today—the life you have the power to change at any moment.

The Advice Trap

OUR LIVES become more of an adventure when we choose to trust our ideas. I learned this when I belonged to Entrepreneurs' Organization, a peer-to-peer network exclusively for entrepreneurs to help them grow. Every year we were assigned to small groups and met monthly to discuss the challenges we were facing.

We shared the good, the bad, and the ugly of our businesses and provided feedback to help one another grow. One of the rules was a practice called gestalt, meaning we were not allowed to share generic advice about an issue another member was dealing with. We were permitted to share only our own experiences. It is an incredibly powerful exercise because hearing how someone in a similar situation handled an issue can shed light on the best way for us to move forward. It was not a guess or a theory about what might work. It was simply another perspective, which was always helpful for our decision-making process.

Belonging to that group encouraged me to trust myself and listen to the experiences of people actually playing the game.

Be intentional about who you ask for advice and who you listen to.

Would you ask your friend with no musical talent to teach you how to play the violin? Of course not. Why, then, are you asking for advice from others who have not done the things you want to do or, worse, are not even following their own passions and Creative Pursuits?

Often, even when asking for it, people don't actually want advice. They may think they do, but what they are really looking for is one of two things: validation or a guarantee.

We want validation because it makes us feel like we are making the right decision. We want someone to tell us our idea is good when in fact it doesn't matter. Trusting ourselves and our dreams is what matters.

We might want a guarantee that our idea will work. Won't happen. The only guarantee is that we win when we try and lose when we don't. It's that simple. Plus, searching for validation ends up being a form of procrastination. It kills dreams meant to be lived and creativity meant to be explored by you.

I almost allowed one of my dreams to die. Years ago, I had the privilege of mentoring an awesome thirteen-year-old girl in the Big Brothers Big Sisters program. One afternoon, while enjoying ice cream and having a fun conversation, she asked me if I had a boyfriend. I told her I did not. She asked why. Curious, I asked her why she wanted to know. Nothing could have prepared me for her response.

"If you don't have a boyfriend, it means you're ugly and nobody loves you."

My heart sank as I sat staring into the big brown eyes of this beautiful young girl.

That sparked a dream in me. I wanted to start a program to help girls' self-esteem and confidence. I did not know how I would do it or what it would look like. Excited to figure it out, I asked a friend what he thought of the idea.

"Who would even sign up for that?" he said with a scowl on his face.

I was crushed and embarrassed, thinking he must be right. Feeling discouraged, I almost let that be the end of my idea. Almost. I still believed it was important and something worth creating, so I started planning the course. I was not sure how to facilitate a program like this, but I believed I would figure it out. The hardest part was starting.

Before I even had a name for the program, I reached out to a friend who has a passion for helping children. She not only provided great advice but also invited me to run the class at a local community college summer program. Were there other programs already available? Of course. But this was different because it was my creation. It was my idea executed in my unique and creative way. I brought friends and mentors together to help create an experience that would make a positive impact on these young women's lives. Together, we created something special. I am so grateful I didn't give my power away and give up on it.

I facilitated Female and Beautiful (FAB) for over five years. Sometimes I wonder where the incredible young women who attended my class ended up. Wherever they are, I hope they are pursuing what they love. If I had listened to the first person I asked or waited for permission, I would never have pursued that passion project. FAB introduced me to incredible women, which inspired me to create more programming for women and girls. That experience taught me how to bring an idea to life. It also taught me to think twice about who I should reach out to for advice. We cannot let someone else kill our passions.

Who knows what your future holds when you decide to give your Creative Pursuits a go? Whose lives will you touch? What other magical pursuits will it lead to?

Your Creative Pursuits are meant to change you in a way nothing else can. It is one of the greatest outcomes of pursuing what you love. One decision leads to another and you find yourself on a path filled with passion projects waiting for you to notice them so they can fill your life with meaning.

There are many ways to find your path to discovering or reconnecting with what you love. For example, Jackie thought she had given up dancing after having three children. Between work, her husband, and her kids, she thought she no longer had time to indulge in Creative Pursuits. She didn't want to be selfish or a bad mom.

Then she bumped into an old friend, Kelly, at a coffee shop. They excitedly swapped stories about their kids and their lives. Kelly mentioned how much she loved the dance studio she had been going to.

"Oh my gosh," Jackie said. "That sounds like a blast. I used to love dancing."

"You should come! We would have so much fun."

Jackie thought about it. It was tempting. She remembered years ago when she would dance into the late hours of the night. She had felt so alive and free.

Snapping back to reality and remembering the endless chores and activities that must be done at home, she looked at Kelly and muttered, "I don't have time."

"You can't make it one evening?" Kelly pressed. "Come on. I'm sure your family can live without you for one night."

Jackie laughed. "Okay, sure. You're right."

Kelly clapped her hands. "Amazing! I'll see you on Wednes-day."

The following week, Jackie showed up in yoga pants and her favorite dance shoes, feeling both nervous and excited. The hip-hop music immediately stole her away. She was transported back to the old version of herself. She was no longer worrying about laundry, kids' homework, bills, or what to make for dinner. She felt energized and beautiful.

She went back to the studio every week. It was the highlight of her week, and yes, her house is still standing, and her husband and kids are just fine without her for a few hours. In fact, they noticed the difference in her. It was hard not to. Over the next few weeks, Jackie would dance into her children's rooms at night to tuck them into bed, practice new moves in the kitchen, and sporadically grab her husband's hands, signaling for twirl and dip. It had been a long time since she had felt so engaged with life.

Figuring Out Life:
Discover Your Perfect Formula

JACKIE FOUND out she can have kids, a job, a husband, and dance. And she likes it exactly like that.

For me, I want a different formula. I want a career I am passionate about, podcasting, working out every morning, and, of course, writing. What does your perfect formula include? It really doesn't matter the combination. What matters is being true to yourself and living life in a way that makes you feel alive and on purpose.

Doing more of what we love opens our eyes to opportunities that may have been there all along. We change after we learn to play the piano, write a children's book, make jewelry, or take a photography class. There is no guarantee that we will be any good at these activities, but remember, that's not the point. The point is the enjoyment it brings and how it helps you become your best self.

You Are Not Your Past

You can't connect the dots looking forward; you can only connect them looking backward. So you have to trust that the dots will somehow connect in your future. You have to trust in something—your gut, destiny, life, karma, whatever.
—Steve Jobs[9]

FORTUNATELY, it is never too late to become a better you. You may have made decisions in the past that you wish you could do over. While we can't jump in a time machine and go back, it is possible to make better decisions starting today. It is never too late to start doing what you love.

Exploring what we love encourages us to look toward the future. We get to take the lessons we have learned from our past and use them to build a better future. We get to choose how we show up in the world. It does not matter how old or young you are, where you live, or what you do for a living, every day is a chance to explore your creativity and build a better life for yourself.

Get in the Zone

WHEN WE are excited about the life we are building, we become more engaged with our passions and get lost in our Creative Pursuits. When was the last time you were so focused on an activity and felt so completely energized that you did not even realize hours had passed? That is what we experience during the state of flow. According to psychologist Mihaly Csikszentmihalyi, one of the cofounders of positive psychology, flow is "a state in which people are so involved in an activity that nothing else seems to matter; the experience is so enjoyable that people will continue to do it even at great cost, for the sheer sake of doing it." Csikszentmihalyi's studies led him to conclude that happiness is an internal state of flow, not an external one.[10]

Creative Pursuits help you achieve a flow state because they are activities that bring you joy. Getting "into the zone," as it is often referred to, is easy when we are engaging in our Creative Pursuits. We get lost in our own world when we are working on a creative passion project that lights us up. What activities get you into a state of flow? How can you start incorporating more of those activities into your life?

Inspired Actions

1. Write yourself a permission slip to start exploring your Creative Pursuits: I, _____, give myself permission to start _____. Sign and date the bottom. How does it make you feel?

2. Identify three activities you are doing because you think you should, not because you actually want to. Make a plan to eliminate the activities that do not serve you.

3. Write your life's perfect formula. Decide what actions to take to start making it a reality.

Myth 4:
You Need a Reason

Practicing an art, no matter how well or badly,
is a way to make your soul grow, for heaven's sake.
—Kurt Vonnegut[11]

MY FRIEND SHAWN AND I CAN SPEND HOURS talking about the creative process. Contemplating whether our favorite authors have a secret writing space, discussing how the best song lyrics are born, and debating whether muses are real. We loved our conversations so much, we started a podcast to share our ideas. It took a few days, but we eventually came up with the name of the show: *Create For No Reason*. Its double meaning makes it special. Create for no reason, but there actually is a reason: Creating brings joy and fulfillment. The magic is in creating, not necessarily the outcome or the creation itself.

Being unattached to the outcome frees us to explore what we love in a more carefree way. Write. Cook. Start a blog. Plant a garden. Not because it will make you money. Not because you will get rich and famous. Simply because you enjoy it. That is reason enough.

We live in a culture obsessed with outcome, production, and results. For example, in business, we measure return on investment (ROI). We decide what to work on based on the outcome we'll get from the resources we expend—which is a good practice. However, it's far too easy for business owners to dismiss the intangible benefits they receive from their efforts. Things like increased team member satisfaction, better communication, and improved company culture—all of which are incredibly important to growing a business.

The same can be true of exploring our Creative Pursuits. If we focus only on the finished product, we end up disregarding the other benefits we get from doing the activity itself: increased energy, stress relief, improved self-awareness, enhanced skills, and becoming more creative.

If you want to grow and become your best self, consider measuring your **Return on Creating (ROC)**. When I say creating, I don't mean only physically creating something like a poem or piece of art. Creating in this sense of the word also means making moments. Creating is spending time doing activities we love. When we do, we feel aligned and on purpose.

A simple way to start measuring your ROC is to start noticing improvements in your life when you explore activities you love. Ask yourself these questions:

1. On a scale of 1 (drained) to 5 (fully energized), what is your energy level after doing an activity you love?
2. How does this activity enhance your life?
3. What skills are you learning that can be applied to other areas of your life?
4. How does this activity make you feel?
5. What are five benefits you receive by doing what you love regularly?

Noticing how you feel after participating in activities you love sheds light on the meaning of those experiences and why they are worth making part of your life.

We can learn and grow from every experience. Shawn and I had fun developing ideas for our show, interviewing guests, and discovering podcasting best practices. We learned a lot in the process. But after about forty episodes, he decided to step away to explore other passions. This is a perfect example of the creative process. Once you start creating, one idea can turn into another and possibly even another. In fact, sometimes the original idea is almost unrecognizable. Things don't always turn out the way we expect, but we get to soak in every moment spent exploring what's meaningful to us at that time. I decided to keep doing the show because I was receiving a positive ROC.

If you are trying to justify doing what you love, start

measuring your ROC. Just because you don't want to do stand-up comedy for a living doesn't mean you shouldn't write jokes if you enjoy it. You don't need to have aspirations of becoming a professional pianist to start learning how to play a few songs to perform at your next dinner party.

What Fascinates You

WE DON'T need a reason to explore what we find interesting. My friend Justin loves music. Writing songs, singing badly, discussing musicians, and debating which musical genre is the best lights him up. He can spend hours alone flipping through his record collection and listening to his favorite songs. Music is one of Justin's Creative Pursuits.

Maybe you know exactly what your Creative Pursuits are. Maybe you are not quite sure. And maybe you are interested in adding more of them to your life. Wherever you are in your journey, here are five questions to ask yourself to discover your Creative Pursuits:

1. If you could spend all day tomorrow doing one thing, what would it be?
2. What can you talk about for hours?
3. What activities fill you with energy even after a long day?
4. What did you love to do as a child?
5. What activity could you not live without?

These questions are meant to help you uncover your passions. Don't overthink. Don't judge yourself. Let your answers guide you to explore your creativity simply for the joy of it.

Justin's love of music is reason enough for him to spend hours at a record store on a Sunday afternoon. It may be exactly what he needs to fill his soul before heading to the office on Monday morning. His ROC is the energy and motivation that carry over throughout his week from such a simple activity.

One thing that keeps me motivated and optimistic is possibilities. Believing that today may be the day I meet someone interesting or have an experience that will change the trajectory of my life draws me out of bed. You are one idea, connection, or Creative Pursuit away from changing the trajectory of your life. One simple activity can change your world. Explore your passions freely. Go on a hike, spend time in your garden, sip a fresh cup of coffee and journal outside before the sun comes up, take a pottery class, bake your grandmother's famous apple pie, write a screenplay, or lie on the floor and listen to your favorite songs. Do something that makes you smile.

The world is nothing but change. Our life is only perception.
—Marcus Aurelius[12]

Creativity Doesn't Have to Make Sense

YOUR ATTRACTION to a passion project may not make sense to others. It may not fully make sense to you. That's okay. Too many of us try to make sense of the world. We overthink, try to predict the future, or get stuck in the past. If we needed a reason to pursue our passions, we might never dance in the rain, take a piano lesson, try improv comedy, or learn how to draw. We think that if we are not going to make one of our Creative Pursuits our profession or if we won't be good at them, then what's the point in trying?

Experiences. That's the point. Experiences that help you tap into your creativity and reignite the passion you may have lost. Experiences that give you clues to what is next for you. Experiences that fill an otherwise mediocre day with warmth, excitement, and laughter. When you stop trying so hard to ignore your Creative Pursuits and instead dance with your creativity, your universe shifts. The world remains the same, but you don't.

If you view your Creative Pursuits as a distraction, they will not get the attention they are longing for. If you view them as your lighthouse, they'll lead you back home to your true self.

It's our job to follow their lead and give them the love and attention they need to help us grow.

Do your passion projects get the leftovers of your energy? We often treat our dreams as if they do not really matter, when they actually have the power to change our life. Sometimes it is the smallest shifts that make the biggest impact.

It's the mother who makes time for yoga and notices she is more present when playing with her kids. The CEO who spends Sunday evenings painting only to discover how much clearer her mind is when she heads into her office on Monday morning. The bank teller who takes singing lessons and notices he has more engaging conversations with his coworkers and friends.

It is easier to sit on the couch and watch a show than it is to pull out your paintbrushes and fill a blank canvas, find interesting objects to photograph, take a cooking class, build something with your hands, or shut the door and write. But when we do engage in activities we love, we are inviting passion into our lives. Those are the moments that transform us.

The Process Is the Reason

The creative process is a process of surrender, not control.
—Julia Cameron[13]

TRANSFORMATION doesn't happen all at once. It happens over time, which is why the journey is the reward. Writers, musicians, comedians, entrepreneurs, and other artists who share their work inspire me to create because no matter how frustrating it may be, they appreciate the journey. I enjoy learning what habits and rituals they practice to generate their best work. Do they wake up at a certain time each morning, listen to a specially curated playlist, light candles, or hang out at a local coffee shop? Maybe they are all part of a club with a secret handshake. It is fun to consider, but unfortunately, creative pixie dust does not exist. However, the one thing all of these individuals have in common is that they show up and do the work. They believe in the process, even when it's painful.

Many creatives leverage powerful routines to fuel their creativity. In her book *The Creative Habit*, American dancer Twyla Tharp describes her morning routine, which includes waking up at five thirty, putting on her workout clothes, and hailing a cab to the gym. She believes in the power of rituals for both creativity and accountability.[14] Stephen King talks about "creative sleep" in his book *On Writing*. He believes your writing room should be a private place you go to dream and that you should get in at about the same time every day and not leave until you have finished your thousand words.[15] Beethoven counted out the sixty beans his morning cup of coffee required. Benjamin Franklin took "air baths," which was his term for sitting around naked in the morning. Maya Angelou rented hotel rooms just for writing.[16]

Rituals help us through the process because they create structure and consistency. When life gets challenging or we feel stuck, we can turn to rituals to provide a sense of control. We may not be able to control the outcome of a situation, but we can show up and put in the work toward our Creative Pursuits. We can choose to trust the process.

Trust the Process

IF YOU want to discover more about the creative process, listen to interviews with comedians. It's fascinating to discover how they think about, create, and practice their work. They get on stage night after night to tell jokes to strangers who are there to be entertained. Sometimes laughter fills the room as if the comedian is a maestro leading an orchestra. On other nights, uncomfortable silence sits between them and an unimpressed audience.

Either way, the comedian shows up and does the work. They share their stories. They explore new ways to express ideas, hoping to make the world laugh. They discover what words to remove to strengthen a joke, and how a simple voice inflection or pause is the difference between roaring laughter and courtesy chuckles.

When they are not on stage, they are writing. They are brainstorming with friends and colleagues. They are coming up with new material.

The more popular the comedian gets, the more attention they receive. They embrace the fans. They learn to master ignoring the haters. They show up and put in the work.

They don't know how long it will take to get a deal from

Netflix or Amazon. Or when they will receive a call inviting them to play a part in a feature film. Tomorrow? Two years? Ten years? Never? It doesn't matter. They show up anyway. They love the high after an incredible performance and the push to get better after a disastrous night.

Get Unstuck

COMEDIANS keep showing up because they trust the process. It's easier and more rewarding that way. Trusting the process allows us to move through life more fluidly. And trusting our Creative Pursuits helps us get unstuck when we need it most.

My friend Ashley used creativity to help herself get unstuck. She is building a business, which can be incredibly stressful. She often complains about not having time for anything else. About two years into her journey, she felt stagnant. She was frustrated, overwhelmed, and stressed. Over the past few months, she had lost some clients, let one of her team members go, and spent a lot of money on marketing campaigns that were not even working.

She felt defeated. Staring at her computer one afternoon, tears streaming down her face, she wondered what to do next. Instead of pushing through her feelings like she normally did, this time she stopped and looked at a painting on her bedroom wall she had created years ago.

As she stared at the colors, textures, and various brushstrokes, she remembered how much she used to love the paintbrush in her hand and the mystery of mixing colors together to make a picture unfold.

Longing to experience that again, she rushed to the store and purchased paints, brushes, colored pencils, and a white canvas. The moment she arrived home she put on her favorite playlist and started painting.

The next day she posted her creation online to share with friends. Not because it was a masterpiece; producing a print-worthy piece of art was not the point. The point was to return to her soul.

She found that when she went back to work, she was refreshed and full of new solutions to the challenges she was struggling with. She had uncovered the secret. Our Creative Pursuits are there to support us during stressful times. They help us uncover answers and next steps we can't see in certain situations because we are simply too close.

Since our Creative Pursuits want to alleviate stress, we need to watch the tendency to overcomplicate them. For example, let's say you have a dream of building a beautiful garden in your backyard. Your overcomplicating mind declares that it will take too long, you do not have a green thumb, or that you do not have any of the tools. These disempowering thoughts most likely stop you from taking the first step.

Your creative mind, on the other hand, encourages you to

purchase the gloves, shovels, watering wand, and rake so that you can begin to play. Instead of focusing on the obstacles, your creative mind searches for the simplest step you can take today. We have access to all the information we need.

You can google "how to start a garden for beginners" to find do-it-yourself videos and articles, and you can get advice from friends who already have a beautiful garden. Taking the first step launches you into action and prepares you for your new journey.

Of course, we must be prepared to actually go on the journey. I was speaking at an event recently. During the question-and-answer session, a gentleman said, "I have a message I want to share with the world, but I'm not great with technology, and I don't have lots of money to buy expensive video equipment. What should I do?"

I smiled and asked, "What is the simplest action you can take now with the resources you do have?"

He didn't answer.

"Do you have a smartphone?" I asked.

"Yes," he said reluctantly.

"Could you record a video and share it online today?"

"Ummm, well . . ."

"It's possible, right?" I filled the silence.

"Well, yes, it's possible," he said, shrugging.

Sure, he may not be comfortable doing it. And it may not be the highest-quality video, but it's a start. He could also write an article and post it, or ask podcasters if he can be a guest on their show. There are always small actions we can take to jump-start our creativity. We do not need expensive equipment or lots of money to take one step toward our Creative Pursuits.

This person had been overthinking his ideas for years. He had spent more time stuck in his head strategizing about what to do than actually doing anything. He had been observing those he admired who had been working on their craft for years. They had professional equipment, a fancy website, sponsors, and a huge online following. He compared his beginning to someone else's middle or end.

We all start at zero. Overthinking makes us feel stuck—but simple actions empower us. One video gets him started. Starting evokes feelings of accomplishment and will fuel his creativity to keep going—to share the next video, and the next one. Maybe people will appreciate his work. Maybe they won't. Maybe nobody will see it. That's not the point. That's not what matters. What matters is that he did it. He shared a message only he can share in his own, unique way. That one video will change him. His confidence will grow. He can use what he learned doing one video to make the next one even better.

It's Always Worth It

You never know just how much one Creative Pursuit may impact your life. When I started developing a true interest in poetry, I wondered what it would feel like to write something so beautiful or profound it would encourage the reader to think about life differently or evoke deep feelings they had never explored. This is what poetry does for me. It transforms feelings into words.

As I mentioned earlier, I started dabbling and writing short pieces but didn't dream of showing them to anyone. I even thought about taking a poetry workshop, but my inner critic talked me out of it. Who am I to write poetry? Who am I to explore my creativity? I'm not trying to earn a living as a poet, so it's a waste of time. Those were the lies my inner critic fed me. And I believed her. Until one of my girlfriends encouraged me to join her for a four-week poetry intensive to learn the craft. I accepted the challenge. Nervous and excited, I contacted the instructor to let him know I lacked experience. I knew the group was more advanced in their writing skills. He assured me I would be fine.

Throughout the course, I got to spend time with talented writers who create beautiful work. I learned about the art of writing different types of poetry. I even wrote poems that surprised the group. They surprised me, too. The experience made me uncomfortable, but it also made me better.

Exploring my creativity through poetry has impacted my life in other ways. It's deepened my relationships with my author friends. It's opened my eyes to a new world of creators.

It's allowed me to explore my thoughts, feel more deeply, and start noticing the world in new ways. It's even helped me become a better writer and communicator. It inspired me to write this book differently. I have even included a few of my poems throughout the book.

I am grateful that I listened to my creative spirit and have made poetry part of my life. I am glad I did it for no other reason than my curiosity and intuition. Short stories and poems live in my computer and hide in my notebooks. Some I share. Some I keep for myself. Some, I am convinced, are meant to be reworked later, after I have given them space to unfold.

The creative process is what's fun. It is less about the outcome and more about the work. More about giving yourself permission to play and explore your creativity simply because it brings you joy. The win is enjoying the process of exploring your creativity.

Inspired Actions

1. Calculate your Return on Creating (ROC). Write a list of at least five benefits you receive when you explore your Creative Pursuits.
2. Decide what you are excited to create for no reason. What actions will you take today to get started?
3. Identify at least one creative habit you will implement in your daily routine (e.g., daily journaling, taking a ten-minute walk each morning, lighting a candle before starting your work, reading at least five pages of a great book every day).

Myth 5:
There's Not Enough Time

Whatever can happen at any time can happen today.

—Seneca[17]

"I'LL GET TO IT SOMEDAY."

"It's not the right time."

"There's no way I can fit it into my schedule."

These are the lies we tell ourselves.

But if you knew you only had one more year left on this planet, how would your priorities change?

My friend Barbara started pursuing her dream of being on television after surviving cancer in her early forties. John started cycling and getting back into shape after having a heart attack. Samantha started traveling and taking cooking classes after her husband passed away unexpectedly.

Each of these individuals has an inspiring story about turning their life around and creating more joy and fulfillment by pursuing what they loved. They came face-to-face with mortality. It was a reminder of the precious and finite gift of time.

It should not take a tragedy in our lives to start doing more of what we love.

Toward the end of each year, many of us think about how the next year will be different, better. We get a clean slate, a refreshing new start in which we choose apples instead of cookies, reading instead of watching television, and action instead of procrastination. We want to believe in this new version of ourselves so much that we disregard how ridiculous it is to think a new calendar year is the only obstacle standing in the way of our living a better life. As if magic pixie dust falls out of the sky on January 1 and pushes us into action, convincing us to procrastinate less and do more. Fortunately, no magic is required to explore your Creative Pursuits. You have everything you need right now.

In fact, every day is a chance to make room for at least one activity that lights you up. How you choose to invest your time determines the experiences you have. Those experiences help define your life.

It is easier to create a life filled with what matters when we are honest about who we are and who we want to be. This looks like making time for things that are important to us.

Often, we don't know what those are because we have spent so much of our life going through the motions and doing only what we believe is expected of us, all the things on our "shoulds" list we talked about previously.

Only by identifying what it is we truly want and what is missing in our life can we start to fill our time with activities that make the biggest impact. It takes intentionality and being with ourselves to discover what those things are.

For years, I ran a goal-setting workshop called Inspired Action. Each month, five to ten women gathered to discuss their goals. The first section of the workbook they received included space for them to identify three personal or professional goals they wanted to achieve over the next six months. From those three goals, they selected one as their priority. Most of the women decided on a personal goal to spend time doing something for themselves. Things like exercising, taking walks, writing, art, photography, and jewelry design.

When I asked what had stopped them from doing these activities in the past, guilt was a word that kept showing up. They felt guilty making time for themselves. They were so used to putting everyone else's needs ahead of their own that they felt bad taking even one hour to do something they loved, which meant they could barely enjoy a yoga class or grab coffee with a friend because their minds were racing about what they needed to do when they got home. This was an opportunity for them to start recognizing what was actually important and stop putting pressure on themselves to do everything, especially things that didn't really need to be done.

To help them get their time back, I took them through a simple exercise that you can do, too. It's called Get Your Time Back. The purpose is to:

1. Identify time wasters and limit or eliminate them.
2. Identify time enhancers and schedule them throughout the week.
3. Help eliminate the guilt associated with making time for what's important to you.

Here's how to do the exercise: Take out a sheet of paper and draw a line down the middle. On one side write "Time Wasters." On the other side write "Time Enhancers." Then, add activities to each column.

Time wasters are activities that do not truly matter, yet easily sneak into our days—constantly checking email, scrolling online, watching TV, online shopping (for things we don't need), gossiping with friends, and other activities that don't enhance our lives. Time wasters also include wondering why someone doesn't like us or why we didn't get the job, or comparing ourselves to others. These activities deplete our energy.

On the other hand, time enhancers ignite our passion and infuse us with energy. They are activities like learning something new, going for a walk, volunteering for causes you care about, reading a great book, or whatever Creative Pursuits you love.

The women created their lists and shared them with the group. Most of them admitted to often turning to time wasters instead of replacing them with time enhancers. When our days are filled with more time wasters than time enhancers, it's an opportunity to pause and make adjustments.

This Get Your Time Back activity was helpful for the group because it shone a light on what mattered most to them and what mattered least. It also showed them in a real way that they are not alone in feeling overwhelmed, frustrated, or guilty. Plus, the women encouraged one another to pursue their passions. All of this motivated them to begin carving out more time for themselves. In return they felt more energized and fulfilled, and were buzzing about the opportunities ahead.

One woman began taking bike rides around her neighborhood. She made new friends and now a group of them ride together three times a week. Another woman made journals with beautiful covers to gift to her friends. Yet another started a blog and fell in love with writing.

Discovering Time Enhancers

MY FRIEND Rocki rediscovered some of her time enhancers after starting a business. She was working harder than ever before and found it challenging to shut down her computer at the end of the day. There was always an email to send, a client to contact, or a report to create.

Constantly working and barely taking breaks left her feeling stressed and uninspired. One Saturday afternoon, after a particularly long week, she felt completely drained. Realizing productivity was unlikely, she decided to put work aside. She laced up her sneakers and headed to a boxing class. Moving her body, shuffling her feet, dodging jabs, and breaking a sweat washed away the stress of the past few days. The more she punched, the more powerful she felt.

To her surprise, she left the class with more energy than when she'd walked in. That got her thinking about how she had stopped making time for other activities she loved—axe throwing, playing piano, and hiking. She had been so focused on her business that she forgot how important these activities are to her. She happily added them back to her life. When she did, she gained a boost in creativity, which made her a better entrepreneur and a more fulfilled person. She realized what so many driven and ambitious individuals forget: Working more doesn't necessarily lead to better results. Stepping away from the complexity of business and life to do something you love nourishes your soul. It's important.

Important does not mean all-consuming. We do not need to find hours every day to explore our passions to create a positive impact in our life. Adding one soulful activity a few minutes a day may be all you need to spark joy and enthusiasm.

For example, I enjoy the benefits of meditation, but I don't sit cross-legged on fluffy pillows breathing in lavender essential oils for hours every day. While this may be lovely for some people, I gain the benefits of meditation by simply taking five to twenty minutes each day to close my eyes, embrace stillness, and focus on my breath. When needed, I also do it at my desk, or with my eyes open while taking a walk. There is a lot of research proving the power of breath work. And it is available to each of us, no matter how busy we are.

You may not have hours every day to draw, complete a puzzle, take a yoga class, or read a book, but you could doodle a sketch, fit a few pieces together, practice some poses, or read five pages before bed.

The Art of Saying No

Taking control of our time also means we may need to get better at saying no. Have you ever said yes to an invitation and immediately regretted it? Before the word even leaves your mouth, you are already brainstorming excuses to get out of it—my kids are sick, something came up, I have a deadline to meet, I'm not feeling well.

One of the easiest ways to get your time back is to say no to things that do not serve you. It's simple, but not easy. Many people care more about disappointing others than they do about letting themselves down. It is important to remember that saying yes to one thing means saying no to something else. Saying yes to someone else's priority means saying no to yours. Saying yes to distractions means saying no to your Creative Pursuits. When you are brave enough to say no to what you do not want, space for what you love is revealed.

Saying no does not only apply to activities and others. Saying no to negative thoughts that stop us from pursuing our passions is just as, if not more, important. Say no to fear, doubt, overthinking, overwhelm, and limiting beliefs. Say yes to hope, peace, strength, and abundance. Say yes to what lights you up and fills your soul.

Say Yes to New Adventures. These are the words featured on a piece of artwork hanging on the wall in my home office. Every time it catches my eye I smile. It reminds me to say yes to what lights me up. Say yes to my dreams. Say yes to experiences that push me out of my comfort zone. Say yes to my passions.

What adventures have you been putting off because you are saying yes to distractions instead of your Creative Pursuits?

Before you say yes to an invitation or activity that requires your time, ask yourself these three questions:

1. Will this help me grow?
2. Will this bring joy to my life?
3. How will I feel when it's time for the activity?

The last question is especially powerful because it encourages us to pause and listen to our instincts. When you book a fun trip or sign up for a class you are interested in, you happily add it to your calendar and look forward to it.

When you say yes to an event you don't want to attend, it's unlikely you are going to feel like going when the time comes. In fact, you may even dread it when you think about it weeks before, which causes unnecessary anxiety or stress. When we are clear about what adventures we want to say yes to, saying no becomes easier.

Pockets of Time Meant for Joy

WHEN WE are better at saying no, we have more space for our Creative Pursuits and can identify pockets of time meant for joy. These are moments, here and there, that we can choose to fill with activities we love.

We may say we want to read more, but because we don't have two hours, we turn on the TV instead of reading five pages. Or we may want to learn piano, but we scroll through social media instead of spending ten minutes practicing. We may love to cook, but after a long day, we get takeout instead of spending thirty minutes in the kitchen whipping up a new dish. It's amazing how five to thirty minutes a day can change our lives.

If five minutes a day seems like too much, try once a week. If that is still too much, try once a month. Start with whatever is possible for you.

To receive the joy of these pockets of time, we must practice discipline.

Discipline. How do you feel when you hear that word? To some, it means strict, harsh, and limiting. To others, it's a way of life that allows them to do more of what matters to them. The more disciplined we are, the more pockets of time we will have to fill with activities we love.

> *Most people overestimate what they can do in a day, and underestimate what they can do in a month. We overestimate what we can do in a year, and underestimate what we can accomplish in a decade.*
> —Matthew Kelly[18]

If you don't think you can find pockets of time, consider Parkinson's Law. It is the old adage that work expands to fill the time allotted.[19]

For example, if there are three days to finish a project, most people will take the entire three days, even if it could have been completed in two. If you have ever procrastinated on a project, you understand this experience. It's having three weeks to get it done, but because you waited until two days before it was due, somehow you were able to complete it in two days.

It's simply an invitation to consider where you are currently spending your time and where you may be able to create more of it.

Jump-Start Your Creative Pursuits

WHEN YOU discover pockets of time, jump into your favorite activities; otherwise, you may revert to time wasters. Something that helps me spring into action is the Pomodoro Technique.

This time-management method was developed by Francesco Cirillo in the late 1980s.[20] It is a simple exercise using the power of time blocking. While it's famously known as a productivity tool for getting work done, it is also a great way to jump-start your creativity. It is a six-step process, but I've modified it specifically for your Creative Pursuits to the following five steps:

1. Select the Creative Pursuit you are going to work on.

2. Set a timer. This technique suggests twenty-five minutes. However, it works for whatever pocket of time you have—five, ten, or fifteen minutes.

3. Work on that activity until the timer goes off.

4. Notice what shows up for you. Write one word that best describes how you feel after completing the activity.

5. Congratulate yourself for making time for your Creative Pursuits.

I often use this technique for writing. I set a timer on my phone anywhere between fifteen and forty-five minutes. I write freely. It helps when I put my phone in a drawer or in another room so I am not distracted or tempted to look at the timer.

Writing for this block of time makes it more manageable, especially if I am working on a big project, like this book. If I spent time writing only when I had three hours every day, I would probably never start. Some days, the timer goes off and I am in such a state of flow, I keep going. On other days, twenty-five minutes is enough. Either way, the simple act of starting pushes me forward. I hope it does the same for you.

It's Never Too Late

DISCOVERING TOOLS like the Pomodoro Technique helps push us forward to explore our creativity no matter what stage of life we are in. Your Creative Pursuits grow as you grow. What interested you in your twenties may not interest you in your thirties, forties, fifties, and beyond. Every decade of our lives is a chance to discover new pieces of ourselves.

It is the woman in her sixties who goes back to school to get a degree. The forty-seven-year-old man who gets his band back together and starts playing in local bars. The thirty-eight-year-old woman who finally signs up for acting classes. The retired corporate executive who writes his first novel.

The grandmother who starts taking dance lessons.

Make time to experience all the Creative Pursuits calling you from within. There is no need to wish we could turn back or speed up time. Choose to do what you love exactly where you are. Embrace every moment. We decide to either race through life or roll down the windows, play our favorite songs while the sun shines on our face, and enjoy the ride.

We are never too old or too young, and it is never too late to pursue what matters to you.

Every day is a chance to turn your life around. Every day is a chance to take one step toward your passion projects and explore your Creative Pursuits. Every day is a chance to do something you love.

Timing Chooses Us

Timing chooses us, not the other way around.

We're rarely ready, but that's the point.

Timing delights in our reaction to the unpredictable—
the death of a family member, the loss of a job, meeting the
love of your life, or a breakthrough that makes you question
everything you've thought to be true.

It's a test of our strength, our courage,
and our commitment to our dreams.

In a complete disregard for circumstances, timing's

passion is to throw us the unexpected and run.

Like a child playing hide-and-seek,

it peeks around the corner, trying not to giggle.

Will we rise up or will we fall?

Timing lives for these moments.

Does it hope we'll be brave?

Does it have a desire for us to win?

Timing has a plan. It's a never-ending game.

The levels get harder the better we play.

Going all in is the only way to win.

Timing hates perfection.

It's confused by our attachment to it. Hope. Trust. Faith.

These are the feelings timing wants us to relish.

Timing has a secret relationship with God.

It knows when to push, when to stay, and when to leave.

Inspired Actions

1. Add one of your Creative Pursuits to your schedule. Give it a fun name. For example, I sometimes send calendar invites to friends with titles like "Fabulous Female Power Lunch" or "Creative Conversation." For my Creative Pursuits, I include things like "Life-Changing Writing Sesh" or "Notice Something New Walk." Name it something that makes you smile when it pops up. Once it's on your calendar, don't cancel it.

2. Practice saying no. The next time you are invited to do something you are not interested in, say no. Notice how you feel. Congratulate yourself for choosing what matters to you.

3. Do the Get Your Time Back exercise from this chapter.

4. Jump-start your creativity by trying the modified Pomodoro Technique from this chapter.

Myth 6:
It Has to Be Perfect

Don't be afraid of perfection. You'll never attain it!
—Salvador Dalí[21]

MY FRIEND TOMMY IS AN INCREDIBLE WOODWORKER. The workshop nestled between pine trees behind his home is his sanctuary. The moment he opens the doors, the smell of wood chips swirled with incense invites him to get to work. He blasts alternative rock, punk, or folk music, depending on his mood. Often, he belts the lyrics to his favorite songs while hunched over his table saw turning a piece of wood into art. When he is creating, nothing else matters. It is where he feels most alive.

One evening, he shared a secret with me.

"A blank canvas scares the heck out of me," he said.

"What do you mean?" I asked.

"I hate not knowing if I'll be able to create the image in my head."

This is such a normal fear. It stops so many of us from pursuing our dreams.

Maybe you have some perfect version of life imprinted in your mind. It's so perfect, you wonder how you could possibly create it yourself.

The perfect version we dream up does not really exist. We may see a blank canvas as empty and flawless. We do not want to mess it up. We know the moment we start adding color and playing around with designs, there is a chance we may not like it. We may be scared others won't like it either.

Only when Tommy accepts that perfect does not exist can he begin splashing colors onto the canvas or start carving a slab of oak to create something beautiful that only his hands can make.

Our life, our future, our canvas is not meant to be perfect. It is meant to be lived. It is an opportunity to learn from every challenge we go through and every flaw we face. Our imperfections make us human.

Your imperfections make you uniquely you. Leaning into them allows you to get more comfortable with your beautifully imperfect, messy life. Embracing your imperfections will lead you to experiences that will help you create a life that is not perfect, but it could be perfect for you.

The Happiness Trap

WHEN YOU focus on what is perfect for you, it frees you to explore your ideas without being so afraid of failure. This means you can choose to find the beauty in the mess while you build a better life.

Admitting that perfect is a fantasy unlocks our creative handcuffs. It allows us to do more, be more, and become more of our true selves.

There is no perfect job, business, relationship, child, body, or work. Being truly satisfied with what you have and where you are in life takes practice. The practice of gratitude. The practice of patience. The practice of not comparing your story to those of people you admire. The practice of reminding yourself that happiness is available to you.

The goal is joy and fulfillment, not perfection. Too often we highlight only the flaws of our situation and ignore the beauty.

We get stuck in the happiness trap. This happens when we overestimate how happy we will be when we acquire or achieve something we think we want. We also underestimate how happy we could be right now with our life, imperfections and all.

We get caught in this trap when we convince ourselves that we will be happy only when we make more money, fall in love, achieve a certain status, or purchase a bigger home. We do the same with our work or creative projects. We overthink and overanalyze before we even start. And when we do start, we agonize over making it perfect, which eliminates all the joy we could experience through the process.

Your Creative Pursuits want you to have fun, to use your creative gifts. They care about progress, not perfection. Nobody starts with an award-winning podcast or paints a masterpiece on day one. They start a podcast. They pick up the paintbrush. Their creation may not be good. In fact, it may be flat-out bad, but it has the potential to become good enough—and eventually maybe even great.

Good enough lays the foundation for progress. It gives us something to build upon. Without good enough, we can't make the mistakes necessary to improve our skills and enjoy the process of becoming better. If we expect to build anything we are proud of in our work, our relationships, or our lives, we must let go of the illusion of perfection.

Perfectionism can stop us from trying. It can keep us from doing the work, so we can stay safe. We may think we need a certain skill or talent before we can start pursuing our passions. Fortunately, doing what you love requires zero talent. You don't have to grow the biggest tomatoes, get first place in a dance competition, win an award for your photography, or end up on the cover of a magazine. Those things may be nice, but all that really matters is how you feel working in your garden, jamming to great music, finding the right lighting for the next photo shoot, or sharing an idea that moves people. It is the creating that matters. The more you do it, the more fun you will have, and the better you will get at it.[22]

If you are not sure if perfectionism is prohibiting you from exploring your creativity, ask yourself these five questions:

1. Do you hold back from engaging in activities that interest you because you may not be good at them?
2. Do you set unrealistic expectations about where you should be in your life right now?
3. Are you only concerned about the end result of your Creative Pursuits?
4. Do others comment on how hard on yourself you are?
5. Do you focus on flaws others do not see?

If you answered yes to all or some of these questions, you may be allowing perfectionism to hold you back you from exploring your Creative Pursuits.

If so, this is your opportunity to focus on progress instead of perfection. Focus more on process and practice than on outcome. Give yourself permission to enjoy the mess and lean into your creativity.

Practice Creates Experiences

As I MENTIONED earlier, perfection was one of the myths that stopped me from writing this book for over a decade. I tricked myself into believing I was not ready. If I were, the words would come easily and it would not be so hard to transfer the thoughts in my head onto the page.

I thought I should be able to sit down one afternoon and write a masterpiece. I did not yet understand the complexity of the writing process. I did not understand that no matter how hard I tried, nothing I wrote would ever be perfect. However, it could get better. The more I wrote, the stronger my writing became. In fact, every time I reread the book, I discovered areas I wanted to change because of my improved skills. I found little tweaks here and there that I felt would strengthen my work. But if I had kept writing and rewriting, I would never have published this book. It would have remained in a constant loop of improvement, never reaching unattainable perfection. I had to be more in love with the process than with making it perfect.

I discovered this is one of the challenges of other writers and creatives. We see the flaws in our work, which may hold us back from completing or sharing it. When I'm finished reading a book or article that feels as though the author was speaking directly to me, I often wonder how they were able to create such a masterpiece. I also wonder what the creator would say about her work. Many writers can point out the edits they would make if given the chance. To the reader, it may look flawless, but the creator sees all the imperfections, which inspires many of them to take everything they have learned and apply it to their next book, article, or other creation. I reminded myself of this so I could finish my book and share it with you. And now I get to take everything I have learned about the writing process and use it to explore other Creative Pursuits.

You get to do the same with your experiences and the skills you build while exploring what matters to you. Growth is part of the creative journey. As long as we are exploring, we never stop growing. Don't let the need to be perfect stop you from pursuing what you find meaningful and important.

Your Creative Pursuits want you to explore your creativity and grow. However, it is easier to sit around and envision the life we want than it is to get up and create it, especially when striving for perfection is drowning our creativity. It can be painful. It can be paralyzing. The person you are today and the person you want to be are separated by a bridge filled with ideas, activities, and actions you get to experience in order to become that person. Part of becoming that person on the other side of the bridge is practicing being on the other side.

Some say practice makes perfect. But I see it differently. Practice creates experiences. Experiences improve skills. Improved skills generate confidence in ourselves, our work, and our ideas. The more we practice, the more we learn, and the better we get.

The goal is to become our best self, not some copycat version of a flawless face on a magazine or social media feed pretending to have life all figured out. We can win at the game of practice because all that is required is to show up and do the work.

The Journey Is the Process

For me, becoming isn't about arriving somewhere or achieving a certain aim. I see it instead as forward motion, a means of evolving, a way to reach continuously toward a better self. The journey doesn't end.
—Michelle Obama[23]

THE LESS attached we are to the outcome, the more fun we can have during life's adventures. Play music, make videos, write songs, or practice martial arts even if you are not any good yet. Trust the process. This does not mean everything will work out the way you planned. It does not mean it will be easy. Trusting the process means you are open to the adventures that come along with going on the journey.

Jump

WE ARE NEVER in control of what our journey is going to look like. The more comfortable we are knowing that, the better off we are. But I like control. It's one of the reasons I don't watch scary movies or go on roller coasters.

When I was young, I went to Disney World with my

family. My siblings rode on Space Mountain, hands in the air and loving it, while my feet were planted safely on the ground as I watched with an upset stomach.

I was never destined to be an adrenaline junkie.

One evening when I was in my twenties, I was hanging out with several of my more adventurous friends.

"Hey, Kate, want to go skydiving tomorrow?"

I knew they were teasing me. But this time I was going to call them on their bluff.

"Sure!" I said with a huge smile.

Their mouths fell open and their eyes widened. "No way!" they screamed.

I said it just to see their reaction. I didn't think we were actually going to go.

I was wrong.

The next morning, I was abruptly awoken by a loud pounding on my door. Rubbing my eyes, I opened the door to see my friends smiling. "Let's go."

"Go?" I asked.

"Yeah, we have to get to the plane in thirty minutes. Hurry up."

They were serious!

They all looked at me, waiting. I *had* told them I would do it. I didn't want to go against my word.

About thirty minutes later, we pulled up to what looked

to be a barn in the middle of an open field. I was introduced to the pilot and the skydiving instructors. Before I knew it, I was zipping into a jumpsuit and listening to instructions and safety guidelines.

By this point, I was shaking. I paced back and forth several times before climbing into the tiny plane. I sat on the floor of the plane, hugging my knees against my chest, eyes squeezed shut. I could feel the plane lift in the air, bouncing like a roller coaster.

I barely opened my eyes until wind started gushing against me from the instructor opening the door when we reached our desired height. I buried my head in my lap, praying to magically get out of this situation. But instead of being transported back to the ground, I was strapped to the very fit, attractive blond instructor.

We shimmied our way to the door until we were sitting at the edge of the plane, my feet dangling twelve thousand feet from the ground. I gripped the sides of the doorframe until my knuckles turned white.

The confident instructor yelled, "On the count of three, let go!"

He had to be kidding.

"One."

"I can't do it!" I screamed.

"Yes, you can!" he yelled back with unwavering authority.

"Two."

My heart pounded so hard I could hardly breathe.

"Three."

I released my grip on the door and we lunged out of the plane.

It took me a long moment before I could even open my eyes. When I did, I saw we were falling so fast that everything was a dizzy blur.

Suddenly I was jerked back up into the sky.

The instructor had pulled the cord and the parachute had opened.

As I hung in the sky, a sense of peace washed over me as I looked at the world spread out in a whole array of colors, motion, and shapes.

"This is awesome!" I screamed.

And it was.

And I am never going to do it again. No use jumping out of a perfectly good airplane.

When we let go of our need for control and find excitement in the unknown, we can discover a lot about ourselves. We discover what we like and what we dislike. We discover what we are capable of. We discover how to create a more fulfilling life.

Overthink

I DID NOT have time to talk myself out of my skydiving adventure. It was unlikely my friends would have let me anyway. But there are plenty of things I have postponed because of overthinking or waiting for conditions to be perfect. Overthinking is a problem many of us struggle with. In fact, one study from the University of Michigan found that 73 percent of adults between the ages of 25 and 35 overthink, as do 52 percent of 45- to 55-year-olds.[24]

Overthinking is a breeding ground for fear, doubt, overwhelm, procrastination, and impostor syndrome. It stops us from pursuing our passions. It stops us from doing more of what we love. We overthink our way out of taking action. We generate so many ideas that we end up doing nothing. Worse, we may convince ourselves we are being strategic by waiting to uncover every detail or gain more skills before we start. But really, we are most likely just scared.

Rebecca was scared to explore singing. She had performed in most of her high school plays and dabbled a bit in college. She still belts out lyrics from *Wicked*, her favorite musical, while driving in her car. But she hadn't performed in years.

Her full-time role as a marketing director, along with her relationship and other responsibilities, did not leave much time for her Creative Pursuits. One day, after getting coffee with a friend downtown, she noticed a sign promoting auditions for a musical at the local theater.

She could not help thinking about how much she missed performing and how much fun it would be to get back on stage. She wanted to try out.

But she worried she would sound horrible and wouldn't even get a part.

Thoughts started racing through her mind.

"Maybe I should take a few lessons first so I don't embarrass myself."

"Or maybe I should just try out and see what happens."

"Yeah. I'm going to give it a shot."

"Wait. Oh my gosh, what if I'm the oldest person there? That would be so embarrassing."

"Forget it. This is a bad idea."

Rebecca overthought her way out of a really fun activity before even giving it a chance.

If you can relate, here is a simple way to stop overthinking:

1. Recognize when you are doing it.
2. Make a decision and take action.

Action is the cure for overthinking. The more action we take, the less we overthink. Overthinking is like grasping onto a tree branch as we are drifting downstream. The bubbling water invites us to let go and enjoy the flow. But we are too caught up in our heads, wondering where it will lead us and what will happen when we get there. We don't want to let go until we are certain the time is right and the conditions are perfect. We can choose to hold tight or simply trust that the current will guide us. Letting go creates movement. It uncovers new places and introduces opportunities that help us figure out our next moves. Overthinking is not only unproductive, it can also be destructive. Rebecca spent hours overthinking something that clearly interested her. She was stuck in **The Passion Loop**.

The Passion Loop

THE PASSION LOOP occurs when we are excited about a Creative Pursuit, but we talk ourselves out of it.

Here's what happens:

1. You identify a passion project or Creative Pursuit. For Rebecca, it was performing again. Yours may be to start a blog, take a pottery class, or play the violin. You are excited because your Creative Pursuit fills you with a sense of passion. You believe it's meant for you. Because it is.

2. You start thinking about what it would be like to actually pursue your passion. You can't wait to get started.

3. Your inner critic starts whispering all the reasons you should not bother trying. It makes excuses. It may say things like "You will look stupid," "You're too old," "It will never work," "Who do you think you are?" or "You're not

ready." That nasty voice can be quite convincing. Often, we give in to it and decide to not start.

4. Because your Creative Pursuit is meant for you, it does not take long for the idea to show up again, which brings you right back to number one. Hence The Passion Loop.

It's a vicious cycle that can be hard to break through. If we always waited until we were ready to step out and try something new, we would probably never do it. You may have spent so much time talking yourself out of your ideas that you stopped considering all the benefits you would receive from doing what you love. Fortunately, it is possible to break through The Passion Loop. Even when you are unsure, even when it's not perfect, do it anyway. Take action.

Take any action. Get up and go for a walk, pull out your notebook and journal, start doodling, take out your phone and record a video, try out for a play, or call one of your Creative Friends—anything that creates movement, shifts your energy, and breaks your cycle of negative thoughts. Make a decision. We can choose to waste time considering every option and outcome, or we can choose to break through The Passion Loop and open our world to learning something new, having fun, creating opportunities, meeting cool people, building confidence, and generating optimism.

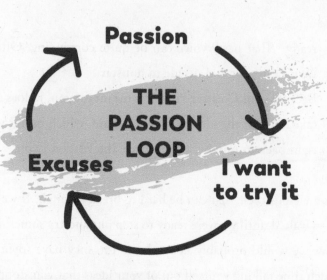

Passion

THE PASSION LOOP

Excuses

I want to try it

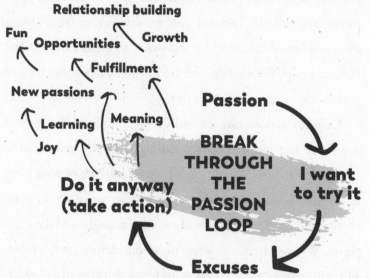

Relationship building

Fun Opportunities Growth

New passions Fulfillment

Learning Meaning

Joy

Do it anyway (take action)

Passion

BREAK THROUGH THE PASSION LOOP

I want to try it

Excuses

Download your Break Through The Passion Loop worksheet at:

ThePassionLoop.com

A great strategy that can help you break through The Passion Loop is inspired by a popular concept developed in business called minimum viable product (MVP). An MVP is a product with enough features to be usable by early customers; it helps validate a product idea.[25] Lots of product-oriented businesses start out using an MVP approach. The feedback received from early customers is invaluable because it provides a road map of what they like and what doesn't work. This gives product owners ideas of where to go next.

For example, Sara Blakely, the founder of Spanx, started the company with one simple product: footless body-shaping pantyhose. Unimpressed with the shapewear options available for women, she decided to cut the feet out of a pair of control top pantyhose, and her idea was born. What followed was a lot of hard work, grit, and determination. Now the company offers hundreds of products for both women and men. Sara did not wait for everything to be perfect before moving forward with her idea, which led her on an incredible journey to becoming a self-made billionaire.[26]

If you don't know her story, I encourage you to check it out. It will most likely inspire you to tap into your creativity.

Minimum Viable Creation

YOU MAY BE wondering what MVP has to do with your Creative Pursuits. It is a reminder that we do not have to have it all figured out to start. We can start exactly where we are.

Approach your Creative Pursuits with a **Minimum Viable Creation (MVC)** in mind.

Your MVC is expected to have flaws. It is the vase you made that looks more like a bowl after taking it out of the kiln, the drawing that looked better in your head than what showed up on the page, or the short story you wrote that doesn't quite make sense. It's the first draft. It's a little messy. It's mediocre. And we don't want mediocre. But mediocrity is the starting point, not the destination. Mediocrity is not what we strive for, but it is part of the journey. It's where we learn and grow. It's where we learn what we enjoy, what we don't, and where to go next.

When we let go of the expectation of being perfect and give ourselves grace, we can freely explore our Creative Pursuits without judgment. Let your MVC be a little messy. Remember, beauty and ideas are found in the mess. Creativity lives in the mess.

And now that you don't have to be perfect, you can be good.
—John Steinbeck[27]

Inspired Actions

1. Identify the area(s) of your life where you most experience perfectionism or resistance to doing what you love. Pick one activity and do it imperfectly. Have fun with your efforts. For example, if you never share poems or ideas until you feel they are perfect, share a piece of unfinished work. Try a new recipe and invite a friend to dinner to enjoy your creation no matter how it turns out. Choose something that makes you a little uncomfortable and be okay with it not being perfect.

2. Give your inner critic the day off. Ignore that little voice making up excuses not to pursue your creativity or trying to convince you that perfect exists. Instead, each time it shows up, write down one quality you love about yourself. Look at this list at the end of the day.

3. If you are caught in The Passion Loop, identify one action you will take to get out of it (e.g., if you want to start a podcast, come up with ideas for your first three episodes and record one; if you want to write a short story, write the first chapter). Keep it simple.

Myth 7:
Inspiration Will Strike

*I don't sit around waiting for passion to strike me. I keep
working steadily, because I believe it is our privilege as
humans to keep making things. Most of all, I keep working
because I trust that creativity is always trying to find me,
even when I have lost sight of it.*

—Elizabeth Gilbert[28]

Leap Before You're Ready

Leap before you're ready. Leap because you must.
Leap because it's the only way to break free of what's
no longer meant for you.
Whispers of fear, doubt, and perfectionism appear from the
shadows, doing their best to draw you in. Tempting you with
the comfort of certainty and playing it safe.
But you know beauty lives in the wounds. It lives in the
unknown. Hiding just enough to keep you searching.
Inviting you to dance with the music playing in the background.
Leap before you're ready. Believe you'll figure it out.

> Not all at once. And not when you expect.
>
> But in a single moment prepared to be found.
>
> Leap before you're ready. Leap to prove you can.
>
> Leap because the answers are discovered on the way down.

Sara came home from a long day at the office. After enjoying a delicious home-cooked chicken dinner with her husband and tidying up the kitchen, all she wanted to do was relax. While walking over to her comfy red couch to watch another episode of her favorite show, she noticed the guitar displayed in the corner of her living room.

She bought it six months ago but had picked it up only twice. She looked at the guitar longingly, then back at the couch filled with oversize fluffy pillows. She promised herself she would play tomorrow, but quickly realized she had said that the night before. And the night before that. Her gut told her to play—*now*.

She picked up the guitar and glided her fingers over the strings. Immediately she smiled, noticing the boost of enthusiasm running through her body.

Snatching the sheet music off the end table, she strummed the chords of one of her favorite songs, with mistakes. She re-did it again and again, convinced she could remind her fingers how to move and get it right.

As soon as she found the rhythm, she closed her eyes and belted out the lyrics as confidently as a rock star. The music swept her away, and she looked up to see her husband standing there amused. She glanced at the clock. Over an hour had slipped by. Gingerly, she put the guitar down, and that night she slept better than she had in months. The next morning, she slipped out of bed and turned on one of her favorite old playlists to figure out a song she would practice after work. All she had to do was pick up the guitar to be immediately reconnected to her passion.

Create Before You Consume

SARA CHOSE to actively do something she loved instead of passively sitting on the couch. Doing so shifted her mood and she felt more alive. It changed her night. Her morning, too. That's what our Creative Pursuits have the power to do. They remind us to follow our hearts and trust that we are on the right path. Remember, creating is doing more of what you love and building a life you are excited about.

Something else you can do to put yourself on this passionate path of creativity is create before you consume. This means putting your Creative Pursuits first, before listening to or watching what others are doing. For example, draw, learn a new dance, or practice piano before watching the news or scrolling social media. It's choosing to be present in your Creative Pursuits and making them a priority.

Creating before we consume also protects us from information overload, which is a tricky enemy of the creation process. It is hard not to become distracted by all the information we are fed every day through phones, social media, and other people's priorities. This content stimulus makes it hard to sit still, be silent, and listen to our intuition.

In his book *The Organized Mind*, neuroscientist Daniel Levitin shares his research showing that information overload drains us of our limited willpower and creativity.[29] When we are observing what everyone else is doing instead of focusing on our own lives and what it is we really want, we can feel discouraged. We may feel like we are not where we should be in life. Plus, constantly consuming leaves little room to create.

Consuming is easy. Creating takes effort.

Consuming more content can leave us feeling inadequate. Creating makes us feel alive.

Sara is a great example. She could have spent an hour consuming a show. Instead, she played the guitar, which sparked energy and enthusiasm. A girlfriend of mine wanted to record a video sharing a positive message. Instead of simply hitting the record button, she decided to watch videos of what others have done.

Each clip made her question her own ideas, until she felt like what she had to say wasn't good enough. That led to her not recording anything. But fortunately for her, she had good Creative Friends who encouraged her to go for it. After sharing the video, she was on fire with ideas and back on purpose.

Creating before we consume does not mean we shouldn't consume great information. Read fabulous books, listen to interesting podcasts, and discover what you find fascinating. Just be sure to discern what and how much information you allow into your world. All the information we take in either helps or hurts us. It can inspire us to keep going or paralyze us and prevent us from creating anything.

I used to wake up in the morning and immediately turn on a podcast to listen to on my way to the gym. Interesting conversations would fill my head during my workout, and on my ride home I would usually switch to an audiobook, or I'd listen to another podcast while brushing my teeth, doing my make-up, eating breakfast, and driving to the office. By the time I sat down at my desk, my mind was so full of other people's ideas and thoughts that I sometimes felt anxious and overwhelmed. It caused me to doubt *my* work and *my* dreams.

Once I recognized what was happening, I started meditating after my workouts, journaling more often, and creating space in my calendar for simple activities like taking walks with friends. I call them "walk and talks." I also love music. Lying on my white couch, soaking in Frank Turner, Lewis Capaldi, Rebelution, or whatever bands are living on my playlists, feels like a warm hug inviting me to just be still or to start creating.

If you aren't sure how to create before you consume, here are three ideas to try. Take what serves you and leave the rest.

1. Limit inputs. Notice how much information you are consuming every day between watching the news, reading articles, speaking with friends, using social media, and scrolling online. In addition to general content, some people also consume six thousand to ten thousand ads per day.[30] Be intentional about what and how much you are allowing into your mind.

2. Create anything. For many people, our minds are clearest in the morning. Before turning on the news or looking at your phone, decide to journal, doodle in your notebook, write a poem, make up a dance, or sing a song.

3. Do a social media detox. Stay off social media for an extended period of time. Start with a few days if you don't think you can do it for longer. Monitor how it makes you feel.

Be Your Own Muse

CREATING BEFORE you consume generates inspiration. Many of us wait for inspiration to start our Creative Pursuits. We delay action, believing some magical force will grab our hands and pull us off the couch or push us into our workshop. But inspiration does not just show up out of nowhere. If Sara had waited for inspiration, who knows how long that guitar would have been sitting there untouched?

Some people believe it is necessary for an outside force to stimulate their creativity. In Greek mythology, the Muses were nine goddesses who symbolized the arts and sciences. Their gifts of song, dance, and joy helped the gods and the ancient Greeks forget their troubles and focus on art and beauty. They inspired musicians, writers, and performers to create their best work.[31]

Today, many people think of a muse as a person who serves as an artist's inspiration. In his book *On Writing*, Stephen King writes, "There is a muse, but he's not going to come fluttering down into your writing room and scatter creative fairy-dust all over your typewriter or computer. . . . Your job is to make sure the muse knows where you're going to be every day from nine 'til noon or seven 'til three. If he does know, I assure you that sooner or later he'll start showing up . . ."[32]

I love this idea of an angelic creature dancing through the world visiting their humans one by one, hoping to find them doing what they love so they can sprinkle shimmery stardust over their heads, igniting more energy and enthusiasm. They reward those who take action. They reward those who create.

Whether or not you believe in muses, consider the idea that action is what generates inspiration. It's doing something that sparks the inspiration to keep going. This means inspiration is readily available to you at any time.

In fact, you can be your own muse.

Here are seven ways to be your own muse:

1. Be curious. Ask yourself great questions every day. Question what you read, what you hear, and what you think you

know. Never stop learning and discovering new things.

2. Keep an idea journal. Have you ever had a brilliant idea you thought you would never forget, yet it slipped out of your head minutes later? Keeping an idea journal helps you collect all your great ideas. Some you may use in the future, many you won't. But they are there to be remembered and pulled from when you need them. You can take out your idea journal when you're feeling stuck. You may even be surprised by what you find.

3. Create a sacred space. Stephen King has his writing desk. My friend Tommy has his workshop. I have a bench outside my home overlooking the water. Maybe you have a home office filled with candles, or a chair on your porch looking onto the forest in your backyard. Find a space that energizes you, that makes you feel at home and encourages your creativity.

4. Play. When my nephews and niece were very young, I would sometimes walk into my sister's house and yell, "Dance party!" I would turn on a playlist as we all ran into Catherine's bedroom to shake our hips while pumping our fists in the air. Create space to play games with friends, joke around with family, or swing on the swing set in the park. Make time to have fun.

5. Find muse mentors. Whose work inspires you? Curate a list of people you find interesting. If it's a colleague, take

them out to lunch and build a relationship with them. If it's a famous author, comedian, entrepreneur, or influencer, turn to their work when you need some inspiration.

6. Go on music adventures. Expand your musical taste by asking friends, colleagues, or family members what they listen to. Open your favorite music app on your phone and discover a new playlist. Lie on the floor and listen to songs you have never heard before, or do this outside on the grass while looking up at the sky. Let the rhythm run through you as you contemplate the lyrics. Music can be one of the quickest ways for us to feel deeply and spark our creativity.

7. Move. Dance, sing, walk, do yoga, tai chi, or kickboxing. Movement generates energy and action.

Let's dig into movement a little further, because there is some fascinating research about how it influences our creativity, which sparks inspiration. A 2014 study by scientists at Stanford University showed that walking significantly improves our ability to come up with solutions to problems and conceive original ideas.[33]

Philosopher Friedrich Nietzsche writes, "Sit as little as possible; do not believe any idea that was not born in the open air and of free movement."[34] Henry David Thoreau also believed in walking to inspire his creativity.[35] Ernest

Hemingway boxed, Kathy Acker was into bodybuilding, and Philip Roth swam each day.[36]

Find Inspiration Everywhere

MOVEMENT CREATES inspiration. This is why the more intentional we are about moving forward and building a life we are excited about, the more it opens our world to find inspiration everywhere. It's an invitation to live our lives with more curiosity.

I leaned into my curiosity one beautiful afternoon when I went to visit my parents and saw a stack of my uncle's old records. Janis Joplin, Elvis Presley, Bob Dylan, and the Beatles were among the mix. I couldn't help wondering what it was like growing up listening to the music of these icons. What inspired them to become artists? How did they write their music? What did they love about their music? What did they spend hours thinking about and listening to?

A few minutes later my mother handed me a weathered shoebox filled with my old cassette tapes. I immediately popped New Kids on the Block into a cassette player. It whisked me right back to the 1980s, when I would choreograph dances with friends and write fan letters to our favorite bands.

The more I played the music, the more memories came back, which inspired me to journal like crazy that night. It got me wondering, where did Janis Joplin write her songs, and what was her inspiration? Did Elvis destroy any of his work because he didn't think it was good enough? Did Paul McCartney and John Lennon know they were making history as one of the world's greatest songwriting partnerships?

Inspiration is everywhere. It's found in interactions with our favorite people, trying something new, lyrics of a great song, staring at a painting, going to the farmers market, watching children play, or singing in the car. It's our job to fuel our inspiration by starting to notice the beauty in everyday living. Notice what's happening in your world.

I could have seen that box of cassette tapes as simply a box of cassette tapes. But there was something about them that called me to explore. It sparked a really wonderful moment with my mother. It also inspired me to write when I got home. It got me thinking about our ability to create magic in the world the way those incredible musicians had. Of course, we don't need to be part of a famous rock band or write an award-winning song to unlock our creative genius. We have the privilege of sharing our own kind of music in the form of our Creative Pursuits.

Notice the feelings brought up while you are listening to your favorite songs, when you rediscover your love of art, or when you recognize similarities in the work you have pursued your whole life. Notice small acts of kindness. A stranger giving money to a homeless man, a friend bringing dinner to a woman who just lost her husband, or a team member encouraging their upset coworker. Let small moments turn into your biggest source of inspiration. Notice the world around you. Notice how it influences your creativity. Your Creative Pursuits don't need to change the world. They are simply supposed to change *your* world.

Massive Optimism

NOTICE HOW the books you read influence your thoughts and habits. If you have made time for some of the activities in this book, you've probably noticed changes in your life. You may have even become more strategic in how you approach each day. I hope you have become a bit more optimistic, too. Approaching life with massive optimism doesn't mean we don't recognize challenges. It simply means we choose to look for ways to overcome those challenges. That we have more control over our lives and our situation than we may think. Building our optimism muscle prepares us for whatever is ahead.

Optimism is contagious. We can't help but love being around those with a positive mindset. It's similar to smiling. It's hard not to smile back at someone who's smiling at you. Even if nobody else is in the room, it shifts our energy. Try it. Smile. Go ahead. No matter where you are or what you are doing right now, smile. How do you feel? The simple act of smiling shifts our mood. It's hard to feel sad with a big grin on your face. It's simple actions like this that generate more optimism in our lives.

Life is simply better when we are more optimistic. In fact, studies have shown that those who are more optimistic live longer, are more successful, and have better love lives. One study published in 2019 determined that optimists have a life span of 11 percent to 15 percent longer than average. Another study demonstrated that part of what makes romantic relationships positive and happy is cooperative problem-solving linked to optimism.[37] All of which help us live a more fulfilling and creative life. Plus, muses are attracted to optimism and steer clear of pessimism. Okay, that is a guess, but I think it's a good one because muses believe in possibilities.

Celebrate You

BELIEVING IN possibilities reminds us that it can be the smallest actions that make the biggest impact in our lives. You are uniquely designed to fulfill a mission nobody else can. Your Creative Pursuits are inside you to help you fulfill that mission. Explore them freely. We can't go wrong when we do what we love, when we make time for what is so clearly meant for us.

You know when you are living on purpose. You feel it in your soul. The more we lean into those feelings and allow ourselves to become the person we know we're meant to be, the more whole and fulfilled we feel. Explore your Creative Pursuits and celebrate every step you take to create a life you love.

Decide and Commit

In Sylvia Plath's novel *The Bell Jar*, she shares a beautiful poem comparing her life to a fig tree. She describes each branch full of figs representing the many beautiful lives she could have chosen—marriage, adventures, lovers, and various careers were all available to her. She ends the poem by saying, "I wanted each and every one of them, but choosing one meant losing all the rest, and, as I sat there, unable to decide, the figs began to wrinkle and go black, and, one by one, they plopped to the ground at my feet."[38]

We can't let indecision stop us from pursuing our passions. One of the greatest gifts we can give ourselves is to decide and commit. Decide the kind of life you want to live and commit to doing what it takes to create it. Any of your Creative Pursuits on the branches can help you create a beautiful life as long as you commit to going after it. When we commit to one of our passions, our muse finds us and helps us build a life doing more of what we love.

Grab one of the figs off the tree and hold it in your hands with great care. It represents your Creative Pursuit. Hopefully, you have already started taking action by doing some of the activities in previous chapters. If you haven't, now is the time to pick one, put this book down, and get after it.

Inspired Actions

1. Decide how you will become your own muse (refer to the list in this chapter).
2. Identify how you will limit your input to give yourself space to create before you consume (e.g., don't check your email first thing in the morning, add creative time to your calendar and don't cancel it, or set a social media time limit).
3. Notice something new every day. For example, open any book to a random page and read that section, go to a museum, take a walk without your phone so you can fully appreciate your surroundings, start a conversation with a stranger in a local coffee shop—anything that changes your normal routine.
4. Acknowledge your wins, big and small. Be kind to yourself daily. Notice how you feel on the days you decide to create first or find inspiration in an unexpected place.
5. Smile. Write down three things you are grateful for.

Conclusion:
Do What You Love

WHEN I WAS A YOUNG GIRL, I had a colorful picture hanging in my bedroom. At first glance, it just looked like pink and purple swirls, but if you stared at it long enough your eyes would adjust and you would see three dolphins leaping out of the ocean. These pieces of art are called autostereograms. They are designed to create the visual illusion of a three-dimensional scene from a two-dimensional image. They are pretty magical. Some people see the image after only a few seconds. For others, it takes more time. Some never see it at all.

I wonder how many people's lives are like those paintings. At first glance, it doesn't look special. We wake up, go to work, come home, have dinner, and go to sleep. It can become mundane and monotonous. But when we explore our Creative Pursuits, our lives change. When we are willing to start noticing what is meant for us, beauty is revealed in so many places we forgot to look. When we are willing to view life through a new lens that invites creativity to be found everywhere, we start to see it.

You have everything you need to live with more passion, purpose, and joy. I hope you have discovered some new strategies in this book to help you break free from any of the myths that may have been holding you back from becoming the person you know you were created to be.

Listen to your intuition. Let your Creative Pursuits guide you to a happier, more creative, and fulfilling life. They know your talent. They believe in your dreams. They want the very best for you. Nurture them so they can help you grow. When you find yourself struggling through one of these myths, or if you simply need a creative nudge, revisit this book for some inspiration and be your most fabulous self. I'm excited for you.

I thought it would be fun to include the first poem I wrote during the poetry workshop I mentioned earlier. I hope it inspires you to share a piece of your work with the world.

Untitled Poem

Back against the hardwood floor
hands pressed on her stomach
she stares at the ceiling wishing for more time

Soaked in music, she closed her eyes
searching for the root of her discomfort

The melody's invitation to live in her head
whisks her into a forest of emerald green

Slivers of sunlight warm her face
branches crackle beneath her feet
breathing in the rainstorm promised by dark clouds ahead

Noticing a small wooden door ajar
she peeks through
Welcomed by long shelves stretched for miles
she steps in to explore

Beautifully crafted snow globes
sit on the antique wooden slabs
Each is filled with moments too significant to be forgotten
A collection of memories

The rain begins and she steps further into this curious place
wandering through the aisles
picking up each moment wishing to be relived
Shiny sparkles swirl around Sunday afternoons
eating grandma's blueberry cake
Dancing slowly waiting for his kiss in the middle of a crowd
The day she surrendered to God

A baby's cry interrupts her thoughts
Walking slowly to the commotion
halted by a sharp pain in her foot
she looks down at the blood-soaked floor
broken glass shattered everywhere

Scenes pictured between the mess
A bride on her wedding day
A mother holding her newborn
Yoga in India, hiking in New Zealand

Staring at a future no longer meant for her
She felt nothing.

Appendix

Journaling Prompts

ALTHOUGH I'VE PROVIDED MANY ACTIVITIES throughout this book, it's important to me to also include journaling prompts. Journaling has been such a powerful practice for me, and I love sharing that experience with others. Some of the most influential people in the world have turned to journaling as a resource to help them make better decisions, explore their ideas, work through stressful situations, and ultimately grow. Former President Barack Obama, Albert Einstein, Frida Kahlo, Charles Darwin, Anne Frank, John D. Rockefeller, Winston Churchill, Oprah Winfrey, and many others have all kept journals.

Journaling is a creative practice with many benefits. It allows us to get our thoughts out of our heads and onto the page, where they can breathe. It helps us uncover more about ourselves. It can help reduce anxiety, stress, and overwhelm. There are no rules for journaling other than to just write. Two sentences, two pages, or two notebooks, it doesn't matter. Sometimes the weight of our thoughts simply needs another place to visit. They have lived in our minds long enough. It's amazing to see what shows up when you start journaling. You may surprise yourself. You may even discover the key to overcoming some of these myths stopping you from exploring your Creative Pursuits.

1. What are you most excited about in your life right now?
2. When do you feel most creative?
3. How do you leverage your strengths at work?
4. What do you want your life to look like one year from now?
5. What does happiness feel like?
6. If you could magically change one thing about your life, what would it be?
7. What is one dream you are most excited to achieve?
8. What advice would you give to your younger self?
9. What new skill(s) would you like to learn this year?
10. What does your perfect day look like?
11. How will your life improve when you make time for your Creative Pursuits?
12. What do you need to let go of to make time for your Creative Pursuits?

13. What are your three biggest distractions right now? How will you reduce them?

14. How do you define success?

15. What's your superpower?

16. What have you learned or relearned over the past three months?

17. What does creativity mean to you?

18. What do you love most about yourself?

19. What do you value most in your life?

20. What lies are you telling yourself that may be holding you back?

21. How can you be kinder to yourself?

To continue exploring how to live your creative life,

get my updates and free resources by visiting:

MassiveOptimism.com

Acknowledgments

WRITING MY FIRST BOOK HAS TAUGHT ME SO MUCH about the creative process. It has been fun, inspiring, frustrating, challenging, and extremely fulfilling. It's a dream I've had for over a decade, and I couldn't have done it without the help of so many people. Some helped me during the writing process; others are simply a gift in my life and have influenced the way I think and work. I am truly blessed.

Thank you . . .

Mom and Dad for your love and support and for everything.

Matthew Kelly for believing in me enough to give me a life-changing opportunity. I am forever grateful.

Joseph Volman for being my biggest fan and making me laugh more than anyone else.

Kyle Sexton for your unique and generous outlook on life and for always challenging me to grow.

Jeremy Pound for your constant optimism and our many creative conversations, especially the ones that last over three hours.

Becca Powers for our many empowering conversations sharing successes, ideas, and challenges during our writing journeys.

Alison Felber for your support and encouragement and for always listening and letting me talk things through. And because . . . sisters.

Kristen Volman for the passion you have for your work and because . . . sisters.

Tommy Kern for being an unexpected friend. I am so grateful you are in my life.

Adam Rosenberg, your faith inspires me. Here's to getting our ladybug bows.

Lisa MacDonald for helping me get through the messy middle.

Julie Broad, Elissa Graeser, and the Book Launchers team for guiding me through this creative process.

To every single one of my creative and supportive friends and amazing colleagues I've met over the years (you know who you are), I appreciate every late-night phone call, walk and talk, brainstorming session, and the constant pursuit of helping each other grow.

To you, reading this book. Thank you for trusting me to help you along your Creative Pursuits journey to reclaim your joy and live a more fulfilling life. Thank you for having enough creative courage to explore your passions and do what you love. Keep going.

End Notes

1. Seneca, *On the Shortness of Life*, trans. C. D. N. Costa (New York: Penguin, 1997).
2. Emily Dickinson, "XXVII," in *The Single Hound: Poems of a Lifetime* (Boston: Little, Brown, and Company, 1915), 29.
3. Marian Wright Edelman, "Kids First!" *Mother Jones*, May/June 1991, 77.
4. Brené Brown, "Brené Brown's Top 4 Life Lessons," Oprah.com, https://www.oprah.com/inspiration/life-lessons-we-all-need-to-learn-brene-brown.
5. Jeanne Croteau, "Impostor Syndrome: Why It's Harder Today Than Ever," *Forbes*, April 4, 2019, https://www.forbes.com/sites/jeannecroteau/2019/04/04/impostor-syndrome-why-its-harder-today-than-ever/.
6. Jaruwan Sakulku and James Alexander, "The Impostor Phenomenon," *International Journal of Behavioral Science* 6, no. 1 (2011): 73–92.
7. Amy Poehler, *Yes Please* (New York: Dey Street Books, 2014).
8. Matthew Kelly, *The Rhythm of Life: Living Every Day with Passion and Purpose* (New York: Fireside, 2004), 3.
9. Steve Jobs, Commencement Address, Stanford University, June 12, 2005, https://news.stanford.edu/2005/06/14/jobs-061505/.
10. Mike Oppland, "8 Characteristics of Flow According to Mihaly Csikszentmihalyi," PositivePsychology, December 16, 2016, https://positivepsychology.com/mihaly-csikszentmihalyi-father-of-flow/.
11. Kurt Vonnegut, *A Man Without a Country* (New York: Seven Stories Press, 2005), 24.
12. Marcus Aurelius, *Meditations*, trans. Gregory Hays (New York: Modern Library, 2002), 38.
13. Julia Cameron, *The Artist's Way: A Spiritual Path to Higher Creativity* (New York: Jeremy P. Tarcher/Putnam, 1992), 195.
14. Twyla Tharp, *The Creative Habit: Learn It and Use It for Life* (New York: Simon & Schuster, 2006).
15. Stephen King, *On Writing: A Memoir of the Craft* (New York: Scribner, 2000), 156–7.
16. Mason Currey, *Daily Rituals: How Artists Work* (New York: Alfred A. Knopf, 2013).
17. Seneca, *Letters from a Stoic*, trans. Robin Campbell (New York: Penguin, 2004).
18. Matthew Kelly, *The Long View: Some Thoughts About One of Life's Most Important Lessons* (North Palm Beach, FL: Blue Sparrow, 2014).
19. Jesse Alan Shantz, "Battling Parkinson's Law," *Canadian Medical Association Journal* 179, no. 9 (2008): 969.
20. "The Pomodoro Technique," Francesco Cirillo, https://francescocirillo.com/

pages/pomodoro-technique.

21. Salvador Dalí, *Diary of a Genius* (Chicago: Solar Books, 2007), 51.

22. Brian Swider et al., "The Pros and Cons of Perfectionism, According to Research," *Harvard Business Review*, December 27, 2018, https://hbr.org/2018/12/the-pros-and-cons-of-perfectionism-according-to-research#:~:text=Studies%20have%20also%20found%20that,clearly%20impair%20employees%20at%20work.

23. Michelle Obama, *Becoming* (New York: Crown, 2018), 419.

24. Susan Nolen-Hoeksema and Zaje A. T. Harrell, "Rumination, Depression, and Alcohol Use: Tests of Gender Differences," *Journal of Cognitive Psychotherapy* 16, no. 4 (2002): 391–403.

25. "Minimum Viable Product (MVP)," Gartner, https://www.gartner.com/en/marketing/glossary/minimum-viable-product-mvp-.

26. "Sara Blakely," *Forbes*, https://www.forbes.com/profile/sara-blakely/.

27. John Steinbeck, *East of Eden* (New York: Viking, 1952).

28. Elizabeth Gilbert, *Big Magic* (New York: Riverhead Books, 2015), 236–7.

29. Daniel J. Levitin, *The Organized Mind: Thinking Straight in the Age of Information Overload* (New York: Dutton, 2014).

30. Sam Carr, "How Many Ads Do We See in a Day in 2022?" Lunio, February 15, 2021, https://lunio.ai/blog/strategy/how-many-ads-do-we-see-a-day/.

31. Aaron J. Atsma, "Mousai," *Theoi Project*, https://www.theoi.com/Ouranios/Mousai.html.

32. King, *On Writing*, 144, 157.

33. Marily Oppezzo and Daniel L. Schwartz, "Give Your Ideas Some Legs: The Positive Effect of Walking on Creative Thinking," *Journal of Experimental Psychology: Learning, Memory, and Cognition* 40, no. 4 (2014): 1142–52.

34. Friedrich Nietzsche, Ecce Homo, trans. Duncan Large (New York: Oxford University Press, 2007), 21.

35. Henry David Thoreau, "Walking," The Atlantic, June 1862, https://www.theatlantic.com/magazine/archive/1862/06/walking/304674/.

36. Daniel Kunitz, "Why Exercise Makes You More Creative," *Artsy*, November 24, 2017, https://www.artsy.net/article/artsy-editorial-exercise-creative.

37. Derrick Carpenter, "5 Unbelievable Facts About Optimists," *Verywell Mind*, June 17, 2022, https://www.verywellmind.com/unbelievable-facts-about-optimists-1717551.

38. Sylvia Plath, *The Bell Jar* (London: Heinemann, 1963), 62–3.

Bibliography

Atsma, Aaron J. "Mousai." Theoi Project. https://www.theoi.com/Ouranios/ Mousai.html.

Aurelius, Marcus. *Meditations*. Translated by Gregory Hays. New York: Modern Library, 2002.

Brown, Brené. "Brené Brown's Top 4 Life Lessons." Oprah.com. https://www. oprah.com/inspiration/life-lessons-we-all-need-to-learn-brene-brown.

Cameron, Julia. *The Artist's Way: A Spiritual Path to Higher Creativity.* New York: Jeremy P. Tarcher/Putnam, 1992.

Canfield, Jack. "99% vs. 100% Committed | Jack Canfield." YouTube video, 5:15, June 17, 2021. https://www.youtube.com/watch?v=r2HBUkbEpWk.

Carpenter, Derrick. "5 Unbelievable Facts About Optimists." Verywell Mind, June 17, 2022. https://www.verywellmind.com/unbeliev-able-facts-about-optimists-1717551.

Carr, Sam. "How Many Ads Do We See A Day in 2022?" Lunio, February 15, 2021. https://lunio.ai/blog/strategy/how-many-ads-do-we-see-a-day/.

Croteau, Jeanne. "Impostor Syndrome: Why It's Harder Today Than Ever." *Forbes*, April 4, 2019. https://www.forbes.com/sites/jeannecro-teau/2019/04/04/impostor-syndrome-why-its-harder-today-than-ever/.

Currey, Mason. *Daily Rituals: How Artists Work.* New York: Alfred A. Knopf, 2013.

Dalí, Salvador. *Diary of a Genius.* Chicago: Solar Books, 2007.

Dickinson, Emily. "XXVII," in *The Single Hound: Poems of a Lifetime.* Boston: Little, Brown, and Company, 1915.

Edelman, Marian Wright. "Kids First!" *Mother Jones*, May/June 1991.

Forbes. "Sara Blakely." https://www.forbes.com/profile/sara-blakely.

Francesco Cirillo. "The Pomodoro Technique." https://francescocirillo.com/ pages/pomodoro-technique.

Gartner. "Minimum Viable Product (MVP)." https://www.gartner.com/en/mar-keting/glossary/minimum-viable-product-mvp-.

Gilbert, Elizabeth. *Big Magic: Creative Living Beyond Fear.* New York: Riverhead Books, 2015.

Jobs, Steve. Commencement Address. Stanford University, June 12, 2005. https://news.stanford.edu/2005/06/14/jobs-061505/.

Johnson, Lyndon B. *Public Papers of the Presidents of the United States: Lyndon B. Johnson*, vol. II. Washington, DC: United States Government Printing Office, 1967.

Kelly, Matthew. *The Long View: Some Thoughts About One of Life's Most Import-ant Lessons.* North Palm Beach, FL: Blue Sparrow, 2014.

———. *The Rhythm of Life: Living Every Day with Passion and Purpose.* New York: Fireside, 2004.

King, Stephen. *On Writing: A Memoir of the Craft*. New York: Scribner, 2000.

Kunitz, David. "Why Exercise Makes You More Creative." Artsy, November 24, 2017. https://www.artsy.net/article/artsy-editorial-exercise-creative.

Levitin, David J. *The Organized Mind: Thinking Straight in the Age of Information Overload*. New York: Dutton, 2014.

Nietzsche, Friedrich. *Ecce Homo*. Translated by Duncan Large. New York: Oxford University Press, 2007.

Nolen-Hoeksema, Susan, and Zaje A. T. Harrell. "Rumination, Depression, and Alcohol Use: Tests of Gender Differences." *Journal of Cognitive Psychotherapy* 16, no. 4 (2002): 391–403.

Obama, Michelle. *Becoming*. New York: Crown, 2018.

Oppezzo, Marily, and Daniel L. Schwartz. "Give Your Ideas Some Legs: The Positive Effect of Walking on Creative Thinking." *Journal of Experimental Psychology: Learning, Memory, and Cognition* 40, no. 4 (2014): 1142–52.

Oppland, Mike. "8 Characteristics of Flow According to Mihaly Csikszentmihalyi." PositivePsychology, December 16, 2016. https://positivepsychology.com/mihaly-csikszentmihalyi-father-of-flow/.

Plath, Sylvia. *The Bell Jar*. London: Heinemann, 1963.

Poehler, Amy. *Yes Please*. New York: Dey Street Books, 2014.

Sakulku, Jaruwan, and James Alexander. "The Impostor Phenomenon." *International Journal of Behavioral Science* 6, no. 1 (2011): 73–92.

Seneca. *Letters from a Stoic*. Translated by Robin Campbell. New York: Penguin, 2004.

———. *On the Shortness of Life*. Translated by C. D. N. Costa. New York: Penguin, 1997.

Shantz, Jesse Alan. "Battling Parkinson's Law." *Canadian Medical Association Journal* 179, no. 9 (2008): 969.

Steinbeck, John. *East of Eden*. New York: Viking, 1952.

Swider, Brian, Dana Harari, Amy P. Breidenthal, and Laurens Bujold Steed. "The Pros and Cons of Perfectionism, According to Research." *Harvard Business Review*, December 27, 2018. https://hbr.org/2018/12/the-pros-and-cons-of-perfectionism-according-to-research.

Tharp, Twyla. *The Creative Habit: Learn It and Use It for Life*. New York: Simon & Schuster, 2006.

Thoreau, Henry David. "Walking." *The Atlantic*, June 1862. https://www.theatlantic.com/magazine/archive/1862/06/walking/304674/.

Vonnegut, Kurt. *A Man Without a Country*. New York: Seven Stories Press, 2005.